HOBBY HANDBOOKS™

BIRDWATCHING

ROB HUME

RANDOM HOUSE 🏠 NEW YORK

ACKNOWLEDGMENTS

The publishers would like to thank the British Library of Wildlife Sounds for the loan of the recording equipment shown on pp 40, Canon (UK) Ltd for the photographic equipment on pp 28-29, Mirador for the birdwatching items on pp 10-11, and Andrew Cleave for the loan of specimens on pp 31, 50 and 61; and the following individuals and organizations for permission to produce the pictures in this book:
David Johnson (studio photography for Octopus Publishing Group): front cover (border), 10-11, 12-13, 17, 25, 26, 28-29, 30, 40, 50, 61. Heather Angel: 12 top.
Aquila Photographics: S. C. Brown 22 bottom, J. F. Carlyon 52 right, Peter Castell 45 top right, Steve Chambers 37 bottom, Anthony Cooper 68, Hanne and Jens Eriksen 57 top, Hans Gebuis 14 bottom, 51 left, 57 bottom, Mike Lane 14 top, Wayne Lankinen 9 bottom left, 16 top right, 17 top, 55 top, Robert Maier 27, Richard T. Mills 44 top and bottom left, 55 bottom, 74 left. Mike Mockler 75 left, Alan Richards 22 top, M. C. Wilkes 18 top right, 38 top right, 69. Biofotos: Andrew Henley 16 left.
Bruce Coleman Ltd: Gordon Langsbury 16-17; Eric and David Hosking 18 center right, 33 top, 62 top, 63.
Frank Lane Picture Agency: W. S. Clark 9 top left, Desmond Dugan 42 left, David T. Grewcock 37 top and center, A. R. Hamblin 15, 50 left, 52 left, 60, Peggy Heard 8 bottom, S. D. K. Maslowski 33 bottom, Francois Merlet 45 bottom right, W. T. Miller 30 center, Philip Perry 30 top, Fritz Polking 29 right, 58 left, Leonard Lee Rue 42 right, Silvestris Fotoservice 45 center right, R. Van Nostrand 9 top right, Martin B. Withers 56 bottom.
NHPA: Bruce Beehler 38 left, Melvin Grey 38 bottom right, Hellio and Van Ingen 19, Stephen Krasemann 54, Roger Tidman 23, Nature Photographers Ltd: Frank V. Blackburn 44 right, Kevin Carlson 35 right, Colin Carver 41, 58 right, Bob Chapman 74 right, Thomas Ennis 30 bottom, M. P. Harris 9 bottom right, E. A Janes 29 top left, 35 left, Philip J. Newman 32, 75 right, Paul Sterry title page, 8 top, 29 top center, 34 left, 36, 51 right, 62 bottom, 65, Roger Tidman 21, 24, 34 right, 39, 45 left, 49, 52-53, 56 top. RSPB: M. W. Richards 16 bottom right.
ZEFA 18 bottom left, 46-47, 64.

Illustrators:
David Ashby (Garden Studio): 11, 15, 19, 20-21, 23, 41, 63, 64. Peter Bull Art: 22, 24, 27 (bottom), 39 (top), 43 (top), 43 (right), 51 (top), 53, 54-55, 56, 59 (bottom), 60, 66 (bottom left), 67 (top right), 67 (bottom right). Malcolm Ellis (Bernard Thornton Artists): 46-47, 72-73, 74. Ian Lewington: 34-35, 35, 45, 57, 58-59 (top), 65, 66-67 (main). Mick Loates (Linden Artists): 9, 32-33, 36-37, 39 (bottom), 48-49. Robert Morton (Bernard Thornton Artists): 43 (bottom left), 51 (bottom), 68-69, 70-71. John Rignall (Linden Artists): 26-27.

U.S. editors: MarthaLeah Chaiken, Ph.D., and Fay Webern

Library of Congress Cataloging-in-Publication Data
Hume, Rob.
Birdwatching / Rob Hume. — 1st American ed.
p. cm. — (Hobby handbooks)
Includes index.
Summary: An introduction to birdwatching, which covers attracting, identifying, and observing various kinds of birds in different locations. 1. Birds—Juvenile literature. 2. Birdwatching—Juvenile literature. [1. Birds—Identification. 2. Birdwatching.]
I. Title. II. Series. QL676.2.H85 1992 598'.07234—dc20 92-11300
ISBN 0-679-82663-7 (trade). — ISBN 0-679-92663-1 (lib. bdg.)

CONTENTS

BIRDS, BIRDS, BIRDS

Birds have been around for at least 150 million years—far longer than humans. The earliest birds probably developed from small dinosaurs. But what sets birds apart from other creatures, living or extinct? They are warm-blooded, like mammals. They lay eggs, like reptiles and amphibians. Most of them fly, like insects and bats. Some even swim like fish. What makes birds unique is feathers.

Feathers are strong but very lightweight. They give birds a smooth shape and create the airfoil shape of the wings that enables birds to fly. They also fit tightly together in a waterproof covering.

BIRDS ARE EVERYWHERE

Birds have developed ways of life that allow them to be practically anywhere there is something to eat and a safe place to rest and raise their young.

Some live among the highest mountains; others soar across the vast oceans. They can fly more than 23,000 feet in the air and dive as deep as 1,000 feet into the sea. They have even been seen over the South Pole. Some species, or types, of bird are extremely rare: only 10 or fewer individuals survive in the whole world. Others are common, with millions alive at any one time. There are familiar birds, such as sparrows, that live close to humans; in contrast, in the forests of Peru, several birds were seen by scientists for the first time in the 1980s. There may be some birds so rare and reclusive that they have not yet been discovered.

WATCHING BIRDS

Birds are attractive and more easily seen than most other wild creatures. For anyone who wants to enjoy the fascination of natural history, they are the best subject to watch and study. There are about 9,200 species of birds in the world. South America has the richest variety, but more than 800 species are seen regularly in North America.

One of the most exciting sights in the natural world is a huge gathering of birds. Gannets (above) nest in vast, noisy colonies; other seabirds, such as kittiwakes and guillemots, crowd together in gigantic, noisy "cities" on sheer cliffs above the sea.

The house sparrow (above) is a European bird. Its origin in North America is a colony brought to Brooklyn in 1852. Also taken to Egypt, it followed human settlements across the desert into all of Africa. Today it is seen almost everywhere. The European starling, brought here in 1890, is a familiar sight from Alaska to Mexico.

LIVES OF EXTREMES

Birds can survive in extreme conditions. In the desert, where daytime temperatures reach 110°F, the roadrunner (top left) seeks shade and ruffles its feathers to keep cool; at night it endures freezing temperatures. Penguins (bottom right) survive on the ocean and in bleak, windswept places with the worst weather on Earth; dense, fur-like feathers and a thick layer of fat keep them warm. The cactus wren hops about in cactus and semi-desert scrub (bottom left). Tropical pittas (top right) live their lives in the gloom at the base of dense, wet jungle.

The California condor, one of the world's largest birds, became extinct in the wild in 1987, when the last free bird was captured for a breeding program. Zoos now have more than 50 condors and are releasing young pairs into a protected wilderness.

LEARNING TO WATCH

If you want to learn how to watch birds, this book should point you in the right direction. Birdwatching is an exciting and rewarding hobby, and one that you can pursue both indoors and out.

One of the most worthwhile things you can do is join the local chapter of a well-organized society. Most experienced birdwatchers will be pleased to help you learn more, and they can advise you on the best, and safest, locations. One of the most important organizations in the U.S. is the National Audubon Society, 950 Third Avenue, New York, NY 10022. Local Audubon chapters organize birdwalk outings and annual bird counts. Many chapters also publish newsletters and conduct activities at outdoor nature centers. Other bird-watching clubs, with a range of activities, can be reached through the American Birding Association, Box 6599, Colorado Springs, CO 08934.

SPOTTER'S HINT
The best birdwatcher is a sensible birdwatcher. Never go out alone; always tell someone responsible where you are going and how long you will be gone. Never visit dangerous places, such as cliff tops.

EQUIPMENT

The most important piece of birdwatching equipment is a pair of binoculars. There is no need to pay a lot of money for a world-famous brand. But neither should you buy poor-quality binoculars with lenses that distort shapes or color.

BINOCULARS

Binoculars use a combination of lenses and prisms to give sharp, magnified vision. Viewing power is described with numbers: 8 X 30, 10 X 50, and so on. The first number is the magnification—things will look eight or ten times larger than they really are. A magnification between seven and ten is adequate. The second figure is the width of the big lens in millimeters. The bigger this lens is, the brighter the view, but the bigger and heavier the binoculars. Try 7 X 50, 8 X 30, 8 X 40, and 10 X 40 to see what suits you best. Small, light-weight binoculars are better. Heavy ones with high magnification give a wobbly image and make your neck and arms tired.

Fold-down rubber eyecups are useful for people who wear glasses—they help bring the lenses closer to your eyes and give a wider field of view.

Roof-prism binoculars are small and light, but good ones are expensive.

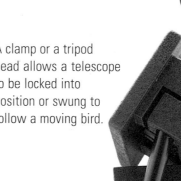

A clamp or a tripod head allows a telescope to be locked into position or swung to follow a moving bird.

Choose binoculars that are small and light enough for you to handle with ease.

TELESCOPES

To identify birds at a distance, birders use a "spotting scope," a telescope with much lower magnification and a narrower field of view than a sky telescope. It gathers light with a prism rather than a mirror, which saves space and allows the scope to be lighter in weight.

Try a 20X magnification and at least a 60 mm lens. Caution: The more powerful the magnification, the harder it is to find the bird in your scope; you see a smaller area, and you lose birds as they come closer in. Ask a dealer for advice, and try out several scopes before you buy. You will also need a tripod or clamp to hold the scope steady.

You use a telescope with one eye. You can keep the other eye open, or close it, or cover it with your hand. Relax both eyes while viewing, or you might see double when you stop!

A 20 X 60 spotting scope, a prism telescope, is rugged and portable.

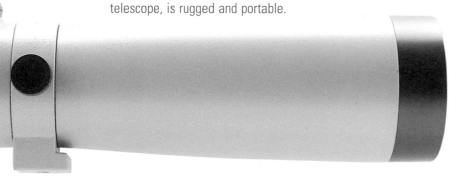

IN THE FIELD

Before you start birdwatching on a cold day, take your binoculars out of their case for a few minutes so they will warm up and won't steam up when you use them. Try not to breathe on the lenses.

If you spot a bird, don't look down at your binoculars and then swing them up to your eyes or you will probably miss the bird. Instead, when you see the bird, keep your eyes on it and raise your binoculars to your eyes. Practice until your aim is perfect.

Always keep binoculars clean. Blow away dust and dirt, and wipe with a soft, dry, clean cloth only when you are sure there's no grit on the lenses—otherwise you will scratch them! Keep the binoculars on a strap around your neck while you walk so that they won't be dropped and damaged.

SPOTTER'S HINT
Never look at the sun with binoculars or a telescope—if you do, you could blind yourself. As you walk, keep to a route that allows you to see birds out of the line of the sun.

USING BINOCULARS

You will see birds most clearly if you use the adjustable eyepiece to focus each eye separately. First look at a distant pole or tree. Cover the right lens, then focus the left with the central wheel.

Next, cover the left lens. Look through the right lens, and sharpen the image by using only the adjustable eyepiece—don't touch the central wheel. Relax your eyes and let the adjustment focus for you. Now both eyes will be focused.

Don't touch the eyepiece again. Refocus with the central wheel as you see birds close or farther away. If your binoculars will not focus properly, don't try to fix them yourself: get an expert to repair them.

CLOTHING

The style and color of your clothes matter less than their function. As you'll learn for yourself, birdwatching is much more enjoyable if you are comfortable and dry, rather than fashionably dressed.

WARM AND DRY

Getting cold and wet is unpleasant and can even be dangerous in exposed places. On a cold day, wear layers of clothing, including long underwear or tights, rather than just a sweater and a thick jacket. The layers of clothes will trap layers of warm air, just as a bird's feathers do. On top, wear a waterproof jacket with a thorn-proof outer layer. Choose one that has big pockets for your notebook and field guides (see right).

Waterproof overpants are heavy and clumsy, but sometimes you need them. Lightweight ones are often not really waterproof, but they do keep out cold winds. Rough-soled canvas shoes are fine in dry weather, and waterproof boots are best for wet ground. Don't forget gloves and a hat. You lose a lot of heat through your head, so a hat is vital if the weather turns cold.

FOOD AND DRINK

When you are out, you are bound to get hungry and thirsty. Food and drink may seem heavy to carry but you will be ready for them after a few hours.

Birds have keen vision and might see you even if you wear dull-colored clothing. It's more important to move smoothly and quietly. You are most conspicuous in white, orange, or yellow—but a bright orange hat or jacket lets a stray hunter know you aren't a deer.

FIELD GUIDES

When choosing a field guide, look for one with clear pictures of the birds. Why not compare some of the pictures in the book with birds you can watch near your home, and see if the pictures are good likenesses?

SPOTTER'S HINT
Take care while eating your lunch, and you won't be cleaning crumbs off your binocular eyepieces as an interesting bird flies by.

READ ABOUT IT

A good field guide should illustrate and describe each bird, its habitat, and seasonal changes. Many birdwatchers prefer paintings rather than photographs because photographs of birds can be misleading. Useful magazines, available by subscription from the main organizations, are the monthly *Audubon* from the National Audubon Society and *Birding* from the American Birding Association. A favorite of birders, especially recommended for getting started, is *Birder's World*, 720 East 8th Street, Holland, MI 49423.

Many local chapters of the National Audubon Society and other nature organizations publish newsletters and bulletins about events and sightings in their areas. Some maintain a hotline (called "the rare bird alert") with recorded announcements of interesting birds to look for and where they have been seen.

ON THE TRAIL

When you enter a state park, wildlife sanctuary, or nature preserve, stop at the office and ask for a trail map. Maps are also sometimes kept in a box at the main trail. Stay on the wide paths. That way, you will cause the least disturbance to the wildlife and will come to the most promising viewing areas.

Maps of hiking trails along public lands are available from camping stores or through hiking or scouting clubs. The named trails—the only ones you should use—are blazed: painted markers are placed a regular distance apart on trees, posts, and rocks. Two markers together indicate either an entrance point from a road or a change in direction. *Never* go alone. Never walk beyond sight of your last marked tree or post. Two more safety rules: Don't go during hunting season. Don't venture onto private land.

BROCHURES

Plan your visit to a sanctuary. Find out what days and hours it is open. Ask the office to mail you a brochure and a schedule of group outings.

MAPS

County road maps give the location of wildlife sanctuaries and nature centers. To find woods and ponds, get a trail map from a camping store or hiking club. Go only in a group with a leader who knows the area well.

NOTEBOOK AND PENCIL

Take a notebook and pencil to make sketches of the birds you see and takes notes on their location and behavior.

BACKYARD BIRDING

You will see many kinds of birds only by traveling some distance to their habitats. Others may be nearby, but the weather might prevent you from going out to find them. The answer? Bring the birds to you.

BACKYARD BIRDS
Most backyard birds belong to species that usually live in woods and meadows; they move into new habitats when they find suitable clearings with plenty of trees and lawns. To a bird, a backyard can be just like a woodland glade. With a bit of thought and effort, the clever birdwatcher can make his or her backyard or garden attractive to neighborhood birds.

THE ESSENTIALS OF LIVING
Birds need four things, which you can supply. They need a warm, safe place to roost, or rest, each night. They need a safe place to build a nest. They need food. And they need water to drink and to bathe in.

A PLACE TO NEST
Some birds will use a nestbox. Others will nest in thick leafy trees or bushes. Ask permission to plant some dense shrubs and surround them with thorny hedges to keep out cats.

Roosting sites are much the same as nest sites. Any thick, dark, sheltered shrubbery will provide birds with a safe place for the night, away from prowling cats and owls and out of the cold wind.

The firecrest, a European bird, loves thick evergreens, whether holly, evergreen oaks, or conifers. Firecrests not only nest in this dense foliage but roost and feed in it as well.

A box attracts birds to nest and lay eggs. Put the box in a safe place, making sure it is well out of the reach of cats and raccoons.

Make sure the box is leakproof and sufficiently strong to withstand bad weather.

SIMPLE BIRD BOXES

These bird boxes are easy to make. The open-fronted one appeals to wrens. Use ½-inch-thick plain pine board, untreated. For a small extra charge, the lumberyard will cut the board for you and make the hole. For bluebirds, the hole must be 1½ inches to keep starlings out. Titmice and nuthatches need a 1¼-inch hole. Put the box together with wood glue and slender nails.

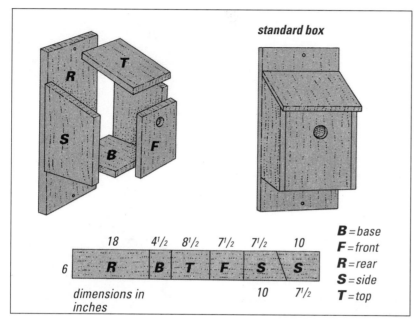

standard box

18	4½	8½	7½	7½	10
R	B	T	F	S	S

dimensions in inches

10   7½

B = base
F = front
R = rear
S = side
T = top

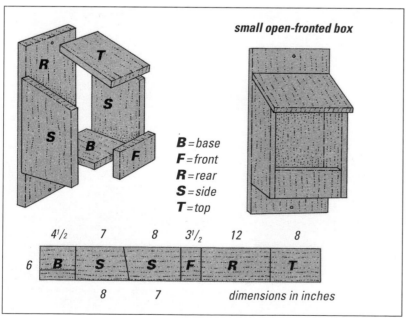

small open-fronted box

B = base
F = front
R = rear
S = side
T = top

4½	7	8	3½	12	8
B	S	S	F	R	T

8   7

dimensions in inches

Purple martins in the eastern United States live in amazing "martin houses" built for them of many boxes on top of a sturdy pole. Purple martins are highly sociable and like to live in large groups. In Europe, house martins build mud nests close together under the eaves of houses.

BARN SWALLOW HOMES

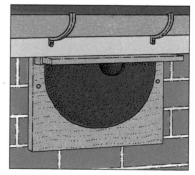

You can make an artificial nest to mimic the mud nest that barn swallows build under eaves. Make it from papier-mâché or gummed paper, and use waterproof glue and paint. See who moves in.

FOOD AND WATER

Providing food is simple and is the easiest way to get birds to come close. A bird-feeding table is ideal for attracting birds in large numbers. It is best not to supply packaged food mixtures in late spring or summer, as some ingredients may be unsuitable for the nestlings.

Water is no problem, either. A birdbath, a pan sunk into the lawn—both make good water containers. A properly constructed pond is the ideal, and on page 19 you can see how to make one.

A bird-feeding table can be a slab of wood on a post. A roof is not necessary, but it reduces wind and helps keep seeds dry. Raised strips around the table edge help keep the food from blowing away. Put out kitchen scraps—cake crumbs, cheese, fat, pieces of bread, dried fruit—then sit back and watch the show.

A VITAL SUPPLY

Birds drink a lot, especially those that eat dry seeds and nuts from feeders. They also need to bathe to keep their feathers in good condition. So they need water to splash in every day, even in the coldest winter weather. Break any ice that forms on a small pool or birdbath so the birds, such as this small finch, can drink and splash in it. Never use glycerin or antifreeze—it will kill the birds.

OBSERVING BIRDS AT THE FEEDER

Take detailed notes of your backyard birds. Count the number of birds of each species you see at one time. Note their feeding habits. This not only helps you meet their needs; the facts you report to a bird club can help to monitor the status of the bird populations. Many clubs issue "watcher at the feeder" forms.

The black-capped chickadee of America (far left) and the greenfinch of Europe (center) are two birds that will readily come to food put out in the feeder. The yellow warbler (near left) is not a feeder bird but will come into gardens with fruit trees.

SOME THINGS TO LOOK FOR

How many species take food that you put out? How many eat only natural food they find for themselves? Do the natural-food eaters visit your backyard in flocks while the feeder birds come alone or in pairs? Or is it the other way around? Do the various birds fight over food, or do they eat together quietly? Do these patterns change in cold or snowy weather, when the birds may get down to more serious eating to stay alive? Are there more males than females? Look at your notes to see if things change in different seasons. Maybe the numbers of different species change as the seasons go by. Who knows what you might discover!

TEMPTING FEEDERS

Some bird-feeding tables are sold with a nestbox on top. These are hopeless. Birds trying to feed chase off the nesters. Birds trying to nest spend their time chasing off the feeders. It is a poor idea! Keep your bird table simple.

Put grated cheese on the ground below your feeders. This helps the smaller birds that are often chased by the rest. Try natural bird food, too: plant some winterberry, pyracantha, crab apple, holly, and other fruiting trees and bushes with berries.

Why not try other feeder ideas? A bag of nuts or scraps is easy to hang—red plastic bags full of peanuts seem to attract pine siskins—or you can buy a wire-mesh nut basket. Scatter two or three baskets around the yard to give several birds the chance to feed at once.

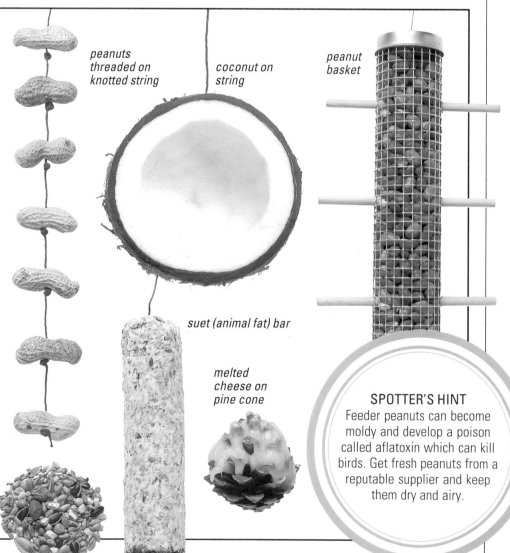

peanuts threaded on knotted string

coconut on string

peanut basket

suet (animal fat) bar

melted cheese on pine cone

mixed seeds

SPOTTER'S HINT
Feeder peanuts can become moldy and develop a poison called aflatoxin which can kill birds. Get fresh peanuts from a reputable supplier and keep them dry and airy.

ATTRACTING SPECIAL BIRDS

Some birds are particularly exciting to spot in your backyard because they are rare or especially colorful. And you never know what kind of bird might visit. It really is wonderful to see something unusual from your own window. To see a greater variety of birds, watch early in the morning, before people are out. A pond will encourage even more birds to come to your yard or garden to drink and bathe.

SWEET ATTRACTION
In summer in the United States, special bottles of sugar water with tiny dripping spouts may attract hummingbirds, fabulous little birds that hover and flash their gem-like plumage. The same feeders will bring orioles into backyards in Texas. In other parts of the world, long, narrow troughs are filled with a sugary solution, attracting a variety of nectar-eating birds in larger numbers.

In Europe, redwings visit gardens in cold weather. They love juicy berries.

Cardinals are spectacular visitors to North American yards and gardens.

BACKYARD SPECIALS
In the United States, eastern bluebirds and blue jays are wonderfully colorful. Red-headed and downy woodpeckers frequently come to take nuts and seeds. Robins feed under the bird tables. In winter, mixed flocks of tufted titmice, chickadees, and woodpeckers roam through wooded yards and gardens.

In Europe, clever use of feeders and nestboxes can attract 20 or 30 species in a good garden, including some unusual birds. Bushes with berries lasting through the winter are great for less common visitors from the north, such as fieldfares and redwings coming in when the weather is bad. Special visitors in some years are waxwings, forced out from Scandinavia by bad weather and a lack of food.

Few U.S. birds give as much of a thrill as hummingbirds. They feed from flowers but will dart in to a special feeder.

A VARIED MENU

Experiment with different foods to attract a larger selection of birds. For example, cheese and suet will attract several kinds of woodpeckers. Cheese rubbed into cracks in tree bark can be found by brown creepers and wood thrush, which rarely come to bird-feeding tables. You can also drill holes in a thick stick, fill them with food, and hang the stick from a branch.

Peanuts in mesh bags also attract interesting birds. Nuthatches, woodpeckers, and other tree-climbing birds might come in from nearby woods. Half an orange, placed on a spike near the feeder, attracts mockingbirds and robins.

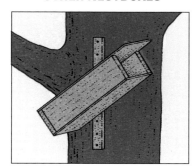

OTHER NESTBOXES

A long, sloping box firmly wired to a big tree will mimic a broken, hollow branch and perhaps attract a pair of owls to come and nest.

Woodpeckers usually chisel out their own holes but will use a box filled with polystyrene or balsa wood and dig out the right-size cavity.

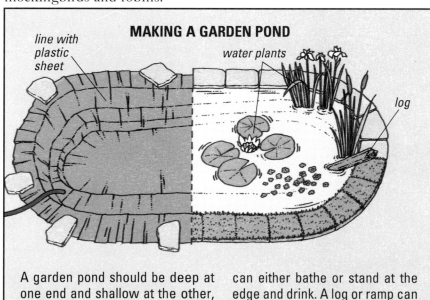

MAKING A GARDEN POND

line with plastic sheet

water plants

log

A garden pond should be deep at one end and shallow at the other, and without steep banks, so birds can either bathe or stand at the edge and drink. A log or ramp can help them get at the water.

The kestrel, a small falcon, might swoop down on a backyard feeder.

HUNTERS AT THE FEEDER

Sometimes birds of prey will take advantage of the congregation of small birds at a feeder. A hawk or kestrel can sweep through at great speed and cause mass panic. If it is quick enough, it might catch an unlucky sparrow or a finch. If not, it may try again later when the birds have settled down. You will soon learn the alarm notes of the birds when a hawk is around. Chickadees give a high, thin squeak; starlings a sharp "tick."

Swifts nest in holes under roofs. You might persuade someone to make a nesting place for a swift by taking out a brick and putting in a board with a suitable entrance slit.

FIELDCRAFT AND BLINDS

Birds have strong eyesight and good hearing. They are under such constant threat from predators that they are always alert and ready to fly off at the first hint of danger. Therefore, to see them well, the birdwatcher has to be careful—and clever.

KEEP YOUR EYES PEELED

If you want to see birds, don't stroll along talking and looking at the ground. Keep looking around, because you will spot birds by noticing tiny movements, hearing small sounds, even seeing the shadows from birds overhead. Look around, look behind you, and look up.

KEEP QUIET

Birdwatching is fun and fascinating, and going out to watch birds with friends is safe and enjoyable. But talking and laughing as you get close to the birds will scare them away and you will see nothing. Being quiet will enable you to get close to the birds and also to hear their calls well. You will be able to hear them more clearly if you stand still for a moment instead of walking along. Remember: stop, look, and listen!

Loud, hissing whispers carry as far as ordinary talk, so be very quiet if you are getting close to a bird.

SIMPLE FIELDCRAFT TECHNIQUES

RIGHT   RIGHT   WRONG

ANTICIPATE

If you see a break in the landscape, be ready to look there for birds. They are often found at the edge of a wood, or where a trail passes through a forest. So whenever you walk up to an edge of any kind, such as a meadow or stream, go very slowly, quietly, and look both ways. Should birds fly off as you approach, settle down patiently in the best position you can find and wait for a while. They often return.

USE COVER

Make the maximum use of any available cover to conceal yourself from birds. If you are walking in open countryside, try not to be highlighted against the sky: it's better to look around bushes and hedges, rather than over them. That way, birds are less likely to spot you. You can crouch in a bush or back up against a tree so that your shape doesn't stand out from the surroundings. Leaning on a tree will also help you to steady your binoculars.

HOLDING BINOCULARS

Keep your binoculars steady by propping a finger or thumb against your face or chin. When it is windy, squat or sit, then rest your elbows on your knees. You may have to lie down to get out of the wind.

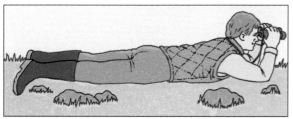

KEEP THE SUN AT YOUR BACK

You will see the colors of birds better when the sun is not in front of you, because most birds look black against a bright, sunlit sky. Also, it is hard to see birds on rivers and lakes when the sun is reflecting from the surface. But you can often spot a bird in thick foliage by looking up through the leaves against a bright sky and seeing the bird in silhouette. Then you can walk around to put the light behind you and get a better view.

KEEP STILL

Birds are especially good at noticing movement. If you keep still, even the sharpest-eyed bird may not see you. But make the slightest movement or sound, and the bird will be gone.

Keep your actions to a minimum. Move slowly and smoothly, pausing often. Be relaxed. If you can't find any cover when stalking birds, crouch down and move steadily forward. Birds may not notice a direct approach as soon as a sideways movement.

Pointing out birds to other people is not as easy as it might seem. Try to use fixed landmarks ("left of the church steeple") or the "clock" system ("four o'clock from the boathouse").

DON'T TRY TOO HARD

Remember, other people may be looking at the same bird as you. There is no need to get so close that you scare it away. That will not help the bird, and you will lose friends, too.

You should also take care when pointing with bare hands, if you don't want to speak out loud: pale hands are easy to see, and birds will soon notice quick movements.

SPOTTER'S HINT
Before setting out on a birdwatching trip, check the local weather forecast. Small birds will stay in cover if there are strong winds.

LURING BIRDS

Some birdwatchers use tape recordings of owls to lure other birds within watching range. Or they make hissing sounds, *pssh pssh*, or "squeak" by sucking the backs of their hands. These strange noises entice other birds to come and investigate, thinking there's an owl nearby. If you try this technique, don't over-use it. The birds get used to the sounds and ignore them, or they move off because they are too disturbed.

Cars make good blinds if you keep still and quiet. You can buy a window clamp for a telescope.

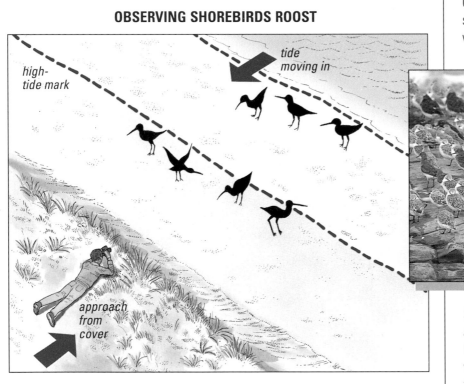

OBSERVING SHOREBIRDS ROOST

tide moving in

high-tide mark

approach from cover

Shorebirds, such as these sanderlings and dunlins, must roost in peace at high tide. Sanderlings need to feed well and double their weight before they fly to their breeding grounds.

SHORELINE SPECTACULARS

Shorebirds feed on the mud when the tide is low, and they can be a long way from footpaths and safe shores. The best way to see them is to wait until the tide rises and they come onto shore to roost.

High-tide roosts of wading birds are fascinating to see. But the birds need security while they rest. It is your responsibility to enjoy watching the birds without scaring them off, because when the tide is high they will have nowhere else to go. Check a tide table for the place you are visiting. Time your visit for the two or three hours before high tide. Find a comfortable, safe spot where you can't be trapped at high tide between the waves and a cliff or seawall. Sit still and low against a bank or hedge. Keep below the sky and wait patiently until the birds come toward you to settle down to roost. Don't get up and move about while they are resting. Let the tide go back out before you leave and have to disturb the birds.

FIXED BLINDS

Some sanctuaries have permanent blinds made of wood. In a blind you can be out of sight and move a little more freely without scaring birds away.

But a fixed blind is like a hollow, noisy box, so don't talk loudly or stick your fingers out of the slots. Keep your hands and telescope inside if you can.

You may find the seats too high or too low. Standing or kneeling may be better than sitting. You may have to stand up at the back to use a telescope or remove it from its tripod and balance it on the ledge in front.

Some sanctuaries put fixed blinds in the best places for seeing birds.

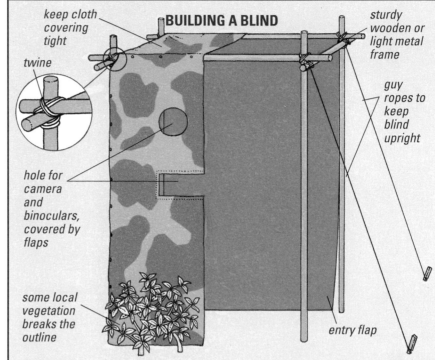

BUILDING A BLIND

keep cloth covering tight

twine

sturdy wooden or light metal frame

guy ropes to keep blind upright

hole for camera and binoculars, covered by flaps

some local vegetation breaks the outline

entry flap

A basic blind is easy to make. You need strong wood for a frame, some rope and tent pegs to hold it in place, and some kind of canvas, burlap, or tarpaulin covering. Rig up four uprights, far enough apart and tall enough to cover you when you sit on a stool between them. You may need crossbars at the top to keep the uprights steady.

Cover the frame with the cloth and tack it onto the wood, making sure that it is tight and will not flap in the wind. Leave one side free to use as a door. Sew on a hook for fastening it once you are inside. On another side you need a viewing flap or slot cut into the cloth, at the right height for your eyes when you are sitting down. Take a tripod into the blind for your camera or telescope. Make a blind in your yard or in the woods, or near a pond or feeding table. It is fun to get close views, even of everyday birds.

The blind must *not* be put near a nest where it will disturb the birds nesting there.

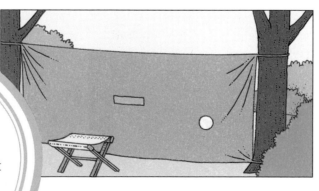

A SIMPLE BLIND

Set up a simple blind with a piece of burlap or an old fence panel. Put out some food and water to lure birds.

SPOTTER'S HINT
Use natural features of the landscape to make your blind less conspicuous—but do not cut down branches from trees to camouflage it.

WHICH BIRD IS IT?

Once you know which particular bird you are looking at, a new world of enjoyment opens up. You can read about what it eats, where it nests, whether it migrates. You may discover things about it that even experienced birdwatchers do not know. First, however, you have to identify it.

IDENTIFICATION

Every kind, or species, of bird is different. Birds can be as different from each other as cats, dogs, sheep, and cows. Some species, such as mute swans, are distinctive, so identifying them is easy. Others, however, can be so similar to each other that they baffle even the experts.

Many birds of the same species look different depending on their age and the time of year. For example, an old swan is white but a young one is blotched with brown. An old herring gull is gray and white, a young one is blotched with brown, and a two-year-old is mixed gray and white with brown spots! And that's not all: an adult herring gull has a white head in summer, whereas in winter it has a streaky brown head. So when identifying a species, you may also be able to tell its age.

FIELD NOTES

The best way to start is to learn the most common birds in your area from a field guide. When you see a bird you don't recognize, study it carefully. First look at its size and shape, then look at its bill, legs, and general colors. Next, look carefully at the colors and patterns of its plumage. Write down what you see.

It is best to make your notes in a spiral-bound notebook. If you make a rough sketch and scribble down details around the drawing while watching the bird, you are less likely to miss an important feature. You can copy your notes neatly at home.

WHAT IS THIS BIRD?

The bird you see here has a round body, short and pointed wingtips, and a short tail. It also has a small, round head and longish legs. These indicate that it is a shorebird. The broad body and small, round head identify it as a plover. Because it has black legs, black, white, and gray speckles all over its back, and a thick black bill, it is a gray plover.

In flight, it would show white above the tail, and strange black "armpit" patches, which would make it even easier to identify because no other bird has such a pattern.

SKETCHING BIRDS

When doing a field sketch, don't worry if it's not very lifelike. Start with an egg shape for the body and a smaller egg shape for the head. Add the bill, legs, wings, and tail. Then label each of the different parts with its colors.

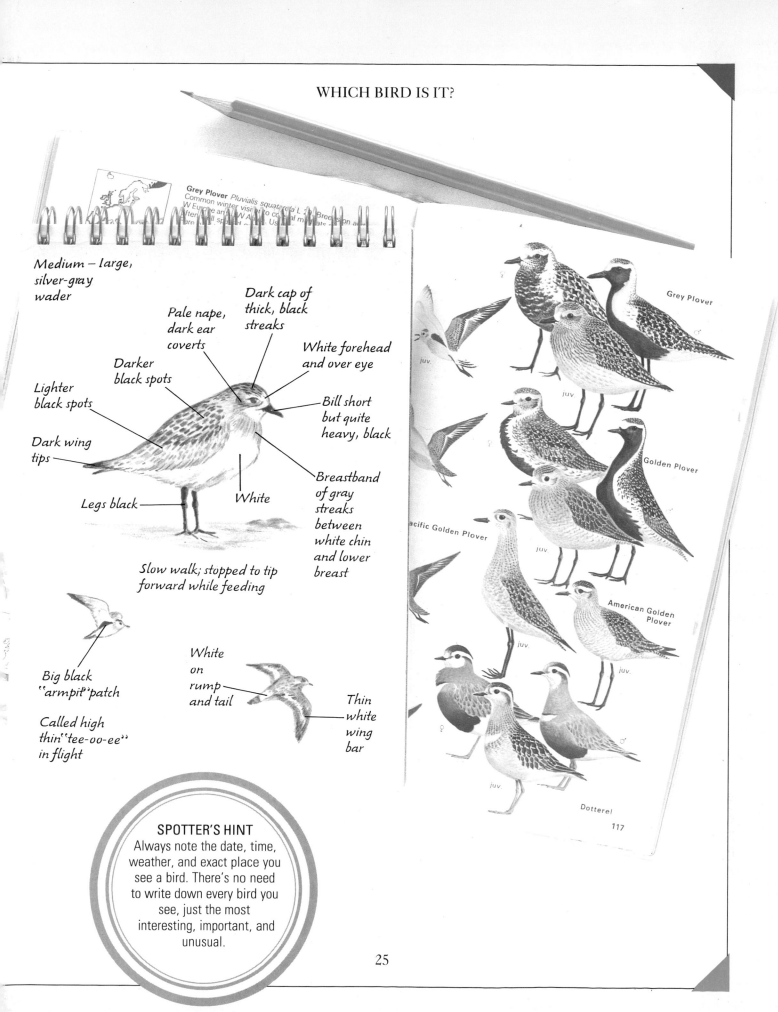

Grey Plover *Pluvialis squatarola* L 28 Breeds on ar...
Common winter visi... to co...al m...
W Europe and ...W A... Us...
after ... will spen...H – ... Us...
...are l... will spen...

Medium – large, silver-gray wader

Dark cap of thick, black streaks

Pale nape, dark ear coverts

White forehead and over eye

Darker black spots

Lighter black spots

Bill short but quite heavy, black

Dark wing tips

Breastband of gray streaks between white chin and lower breast

Legs black

White

Slow walk; stopped to tip forward while feeding

Big black "armpit" patch

White on rump and tail

Thin white wing bar

Called high thin "tee-oo-ee" in flight

Grey Plover

juv.

Golden Plover

Pacific Golden Plover

juv.

American Golden Plover

juv.

juv.

Dotterel

117

SPOTTER'S HINT
Always note the date, time, weather, and exact place you see a bird. There's no need to write down every bird you see, just the most interesting, important, and unusual.

25

FIELD GUIDES

It is important to be patient and careful when you use a field guide, otherwise you can easily make mistakes. Don't just select the first bird that looks a bit like the one you saw. Read about its plumage, calls, and habits, too, and check the distribution maps—it would be foolish to identify a bird that should be thousands of miles away at that time of year!

A PRIVATE BIRD DIARY

A bird diary should do two jobs. First, keep your notes in day-to-day order, so you can recall where you've been and what you saw on each particular day. This arrangement will also help you to see the comings and goings of different birds throughout the seasons. If you keep a real diary, you can also see who you were with and what the weather was like. You can include sketches and photographs.

But if you only have a day-to-day diary and you want to look up your notes on a particular species, you will have to leaf through pages and pages.

The solution is to keep a daily diary *and* a separate card index for the most interesting birds. Arrange the cards in the same order as the birds in your field guide.

Good records help you make better use of your birdwatching observations. A card index keeps things in order.

FIELD MARKS

The special features of a bird—those that help you identify it—are called its field marks. Some birds have lines across the wing, called *wing bars*, or stripes across the eyes, called *eye stripes*. Many birds have white on the sides of their tail, or *white outer tail feathers*. Other birds have streaks or spots or color patches on various parts of the body. Knowing the names for the parts of a bird helps you to take notes and understand the descriptions of field marks in the guidebooks.

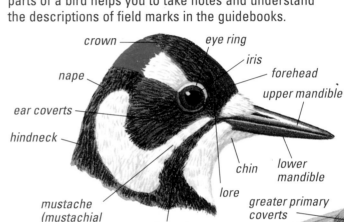

crown — eye ring — iris — forehead — upper mandible — nape — ear coverts — hindneck — chin — lower mandible — lore — mustache (mustachial stripe) — malar stripe — greater primary coverts — primaries

SPOTTER'S HINT
Study your notes to spot patterns of behavior in a seasonal bird. For example, you might find more shorebirds at a lake after the heat of summer, when water levels are low.

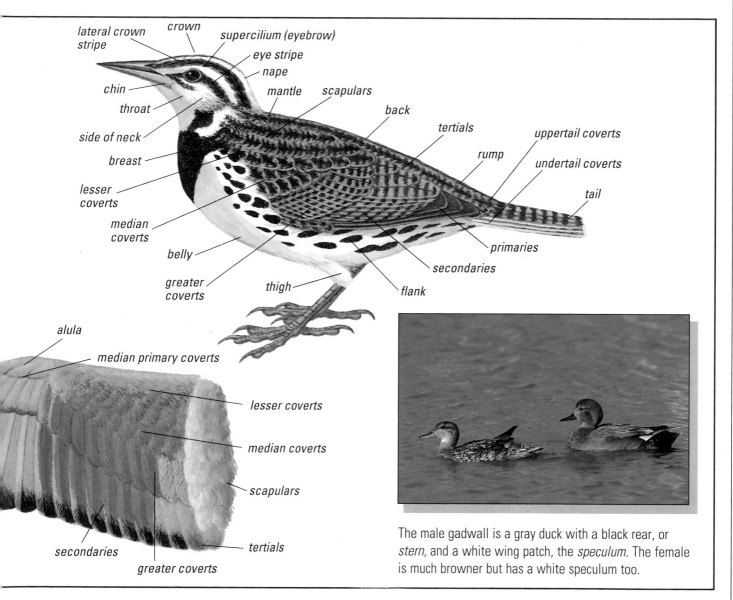

lateral crown stripe
crown
supercilium (eyebrow)
eye stripe
nape
mantle
scapulars
back
tertials
rump
uppertail coverts
undertail coverts
tail
chin
throat
side of neck
breast
lesser coverts
median coverts
belly
greater coverts
thigh
flank
secondaries
primaries

alula
median primary coverts
lesser coverts
median coverts
scapulars
tertials
secondaries
greater coverts

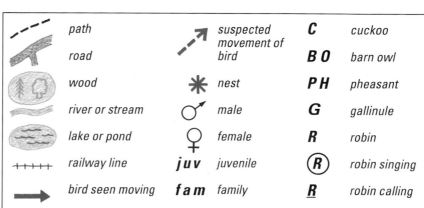

The male gadwall is a gray duck with a black rear, or *stern,* and a white wing patch, the *speculum.* The female is much browner but has a white speculum too.

MAPPING BIRD SIGHTINGS

Birdwatchers use standard symbols in their notes and on maps to represent birds they have seen or heard so that others can understand their records. You can use the same codes and symbols in your notes. When conducting a census, or official count, of the numbers of breeding birds, birdwatchers mark these symbols in the appropriate place on a map.

Symbol	Meaning	Symbol	Meaning	Code	Meaning
– – –	path	↗	suspected movement of bird	*C*	cuckoo
	road	✳	nest	*B O*	barn owl
	wood			*P H*	pheasant
	river or stream	♂	male	*G*	gallinule
	lake or pond	♀	female	*R*	robin
+++++	railway line	*juv*	juvenile	ⓡ	robin singing
→	bird seen moving	*fam*	family	R̲	robin calling

BETTER BIRD PHOTOGRAPHY

Taking pictures of birds is not too difficult. Taking *good* pictures of birds, however, is difficult indeed! The way to become a good photographer is to practice and learn from your mistakes.

PRACTICE MAKES PERFECT

It is good fun to try taking photographs of birds, but don't expect great results right away. You have to be patient. You need plenty of time and good equipment. Photography isn't a cheap hobby. A good camera is expensive, and film and printing are costly, too.

If you think you might be interested, try to borrow a camera or consider some secondhand ones before buying expensive equipment. That way, you can see whether you really enjoy bird photography or would rather concentrate on just watching the birds.

Having decided that bird photography is for you, don't rush out and buy the first camera that you see. Compare the features of different models to find the most suitable for your needs: one you can use comfortably and that will take good shots.

Sometimes a dealer will let you take some test shots to see what sort of results you get.

LOOKING THROUGH THE LENS

To take good photographs, you need a single-lens reflex (SLR) camera with interchangeable lenses. Single-lens reflex means that light entering the lens strikes a mirror that reflects it through the eyepiece. So when you look through the camera, you see the exact picture that the camera will take.

With an SLR camera, you can fit a range of telephoto lenses to magnify the picture of the bird without having to move any closer.

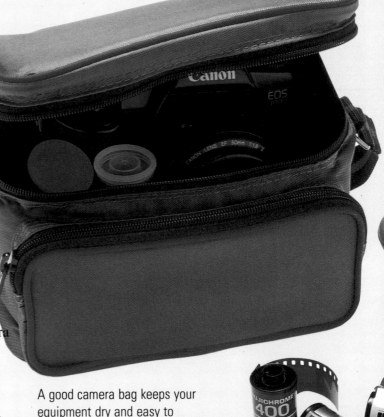

A good camera bag keeps your equipment dry and easy to find in a hurry.

Cameras are expensive, but it's worth buying the best you can afford. Many dealers sell excellent second-hand cameras.

Try several types of film and see which you prefer. Film costs a lot, but why spoil your efforts with poor materials?

A tripod helps steady your camera. It is vital if you use a long lens.

If you have a blind, you can use a 200 mm or 300 mm lens, which will give you a reasonable level of magnification. Without a blind, you have to take pictures from farther away, so you may need longer lenses—perhaps powerful 400 mm or 500 mm ones. These are heavy and expensive, but you can't do long-distance photography without them, except for pictures of flocks of birds.

A 50 mm lens is of little use for small birds.

A 600 mm lens makes birds look much bigger.

A good lens will make all the difference. With high magnification it will give you the close-ups you want. Your camera and lenses can last a lifetime if treated carefully.

SPOTTER'S HINT
To use a long lens, mount the camera on a tripod; otherwise the lens will shake and wobble. The tiniest movement—one you can't even see—can blur your picture.

THE RIGHT FILM

You need slow film for very good quality pictures, but it is easier to take photos with fast film. Fast film means you can use a faster shutter speed to photograph a moving bird. Fast film also lets you take pictures in duller light. But it gives a coarser, grainy image. Bearing this in mind, you need to use the slowest film you can under the prevailing conditions. Try ASA 64 or ASA 100, both slow films. If you use the faster ASA 200 film, the pictures may still be okay; ASA 400 or ASA 1000 will give poorer results.

Professionals often use color transparency (slide) film. The pictures in this book were taken on slides. But prints can be mounted in your bird diary or shown to friends without a projector.

Slow film gives a sharper picture.

Fast film catches the action without blurring.

ON LOCATION

Don't take pictures of birds, chicks, or eggs at a nest. Even when you don't see the parents, at least one is always nearby, and you might cause them to abandon the nest. Only an expert bird photographer can do the job properly, usually by concealing remote-controlled equipment at a bird station before the breeding season. The first rule of the bird photographer is, the birds come first: No photo is worth frightening a bird away from its eggs or nestlings. Photograph birds from your backyard feeder, the edge of a pond, or a brook in the woods. Make sure there is some sunlight. It is hard to get a good picture in dark woods.

TAKING TO THE AIR

Most birds fly, and many show an astonishing mastery of the air, spending the majority of their lives aloft. The young swift, for example, may fly for three years before landing for the first time!

STRONG AND LIGHT

Birds' bones are sturdy but very light. They are hollow and have internal struts, which saves weight but maintains strength. They can support long feathers on long wings. Airplanes and racing cars are built in the same way.

The flight feathers are also strong. A central shaft stiffens each feather, and the big feathers on the wing push powerfully against the air and move the bird along. As the bird moves forward, the air is forced by the airfoil shape of the wing to travel farther, and therefore faster, over the top. This creates lower air pressure above the wing than below, so the bird is pushed upward: it gains "lift."

EFFECTIVE MUSCLE

Big muscles attached to the breastbone of a bird pull the wings downward. The bird's heart is strong and beats very fast, pumping the blood, which is full of oxygen picked up from strong lungs. This gives the bird an enormous amount of energy, helping it to get airborne and to move quickly over long distances.

SOARING ON AIR

Some birds have slight bodies and long, narrow wings. They don't fly by beating their wings a great deal, but by gliding. Albatrosses glide on the air currents that rise off the slopes of ocean waves. Eagles soar on the wind that sweeps up above mountain cliffs. Vultures ride on "bubbles" of hot air that form each morning in hot areas over land. All of these birds glide without using up precious energy.

Birds of prey have "fingers" at their wingtips: The edges of their feathers are cut away, leaving slots between them. These slots reduce turbulence at the wingtip, making the birds extremely stable in the air. Airplanes copy this stabilizing device.

The tail is used as a rudder to steer a bird in flight. A tern (left) or kite twists its forked tail to gain extra agility.

Swans have to take off from water. They run along the surface to get up enough speed for lift-off.

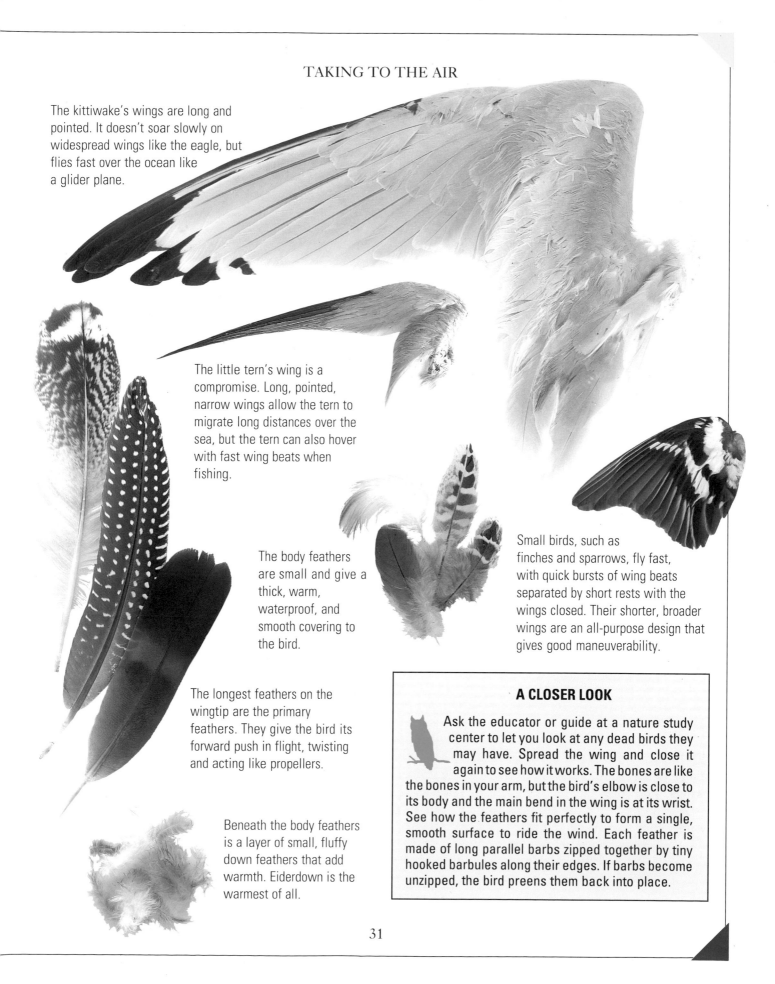

The kittiwake's wings are long and pointed. It doesn't soar slowly on widespread wings like the eagle, but flies fast over the ocean like a glider plane.

The little tern's wing is a compromise. Long, pointed, narrow wings allow the tern to migrate long distances over the sea, but the tern can also hover with fast wing beats when fishing.

The body feathers are small and give a thick, warm, waterproof, and smooth covering to the bird.

Small birds, such as finches and sparrows, fly fast, with quick bursts of wing beats separated by short rests with the wings closed. Their shorter, broader wings are an all-purpose design that gives good maneuverability.

The longest feathers on the wingtip are the primary feathers. They give the bird its forward push in flight, twisting and acting like propellers.

Beneath the body feathers is a layer of small, fluffy down feathers that add warmth. Eiderdown is the warmest of all.

A CLOSER LOOK

Ask the educator or guide at a nature study center to let you look at any dead birds they may have. Spread the wing and close it again to see how it works. The bones are like the bones in your arm, but the bird's elbow is close to its body and the main bend in the wing is at its wrist. See how the feathers fit perfectly to form a single, smooth surface to ride the wind. Each feather is made of long parallel barbs zipped together by tiny hooked barbules along their edges. If barbs become unzipped, the bird preens them back into place.

PLUMES AND PATTERNS

Birds' feathers come in all shapes and colors and have many uses, such as hiding the bird or enabling it to attract attention.

Dull or patterned feathers can give a bird good camouflage, just like a soldier's field uniform. Not all camouflage has to be dull, though. It can break up a bird's outline by being a mixture of strong colors or patterns of black and white. If the bird keeps still, the pattern makes its shape hard to pick out. Masters of camouflage, such as the woodcock, are perfect mimics of dead leaves and grasses. They have beautiful and detailed color schemes. Bitterns have striped feathers, and when they stand upright they look just like the reeds in which they live.

The ringed plover sits on its nest in stones and seashells. Its black and white pattern makes it invisible in the light and shade of the pebbles.

SHOWING OFF

Bright colors are used to attract attention. Male birds need to attract females or drive off other males. They do both with bright feathers, strong colors, or strange shapes. The most famous show-off is the peacock. Other examples are the egret, with its long, wispy plumes like the foliage of weeping willows, and the ruff, with special ear tufts and colorful adornments on its neck. Even common pheasants have shiny, strikingly patterned plumage and long tails.

CHANGING WITH AGE

Gulls are brownish when they are young. Because they don't look like adult gulls, which are white, they run less risk of being attacked as rivals by older birds. They turn whiter as they become old enough to fight for a territory and a mate. In a herring gull colony, you can tell by the differences in plumage which birds are in their first, second, or third year, and which are older. Age differences are usually harder to observe in other birds.

1st winter

2nd winter

3rd winter

adult breeding

adult winter

juvenile

adult breeding

Mediterranean subspecies

Seabirds such as the sooty tern are dark on top, so they are not easily seen from above by predators. They are white underneath and along the front of their wings and forehead, and this makes them hard to see from underwater against the sky when they are scouting for fish.

By looking at the amount of purple and blue in its feathering, you can tell whether an indigo bunting is a male or female, and roughly how old it is; the bluest are old males.

MOLT

Birds' feathers last only about a year. They are completely replaced, usually before migration, in a process called molting. When a bird molts, each feather gradually loosens, falls out, and is replaced. If all the feathers were to fall out at once, the bird would not be able to fly or keep warm and would soon die.

Each bird species has its own molting pattern. The larger feathers fall out in the same order and at the same time each year. Wing feathers take the longest to molt, because one feather is replaced before the next one falls out. But some water birds, including ducks, geese, swans, and grebes, lose all their wing feathers at once and can't fly for a while.

The shimmering colors of the kingfisher's feathers come from light reflecting off the surface of the feathers themselves. The other source of color in birds' feathers is pigment in the cells.

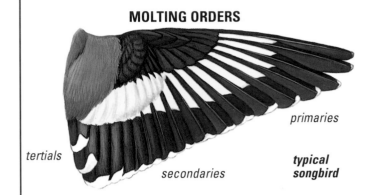

MOLTING ORDERS

tertials   *secondaries*   *primaries*   **typical songbird**

Birds' feathers are replaced in a regular sequence. This is always the same for a particular species. Most songbirds start from the innermost primary, working out, and from the outermost secondary inward.

For a short time each summer, the male mallard loses his striking plumage and looks more like the female.

COLORS ECLIPSED

Male mallards are usually bright and gaudy. They display to each other and show off to females. The females are dull and brown. They have to sit in the nest for several weeks until the eggs hatch, so they must be well camouflaged.

In late summer, male ducks have a duller, darker plumage for a few weeks, coinciding with their molt. This is called the eclipse. It is the duck's non-breeding plumage. Courtship and mating take place during the winter and spring.

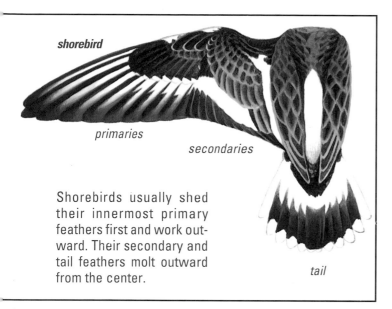

shorebird

primaries

secondaries

Shorebirds usually shed their innermost primary feathers first and work outward. Their secondary and tail feathers molt outward from the center.

tail

CHANGING WITH THE SEASONS

During a molt, changes in color are gradual because feathers are never replaced all at once. The changes often follow the seasons of the year. The ptarmigan turns white in winter, when it lives in deep snow. In spring it becomes patchy white and gray. By summer, after the snow has melted, it has changed to brown and matches the speckled rocks and lichens.

Chaffinches have brown heads in the winter. In spring, the pale brown tips of the feathers suddenly break up and fall away. Underneath is revealed a bright blue-gray. The chaffinch has changed color without changing any feathers!

Snowy owls are white and can hide in a snowy landscape. They aren't hiding from predators, as ptarmigans do, but are keeping out of sight of their prey. They use their camouflage for hunting, not for defense.

Wheatears have plumage that is eye-catching in a photo. But on the rocky slope of a mountain, the black, white, and gray shades are lost against the background, and the bird is protected from keen-eyed predators.

DISPLAY AND SONGFLIGHT

Display is simply showing off. It is used by male birds to attract females. And when birds need to defend their living space from intruders, display takes the place of real fighting.

COURTSHIP

Trying to find a mate and establish a relationship is the main reason for many displays and songs. Some birds pair with the same mates for their entire lives, but most pair up for just one summer. Some don't stay together at all—one male mates with all the females and then scoots off—and these males often have the strangest displays. Typical of the one-season pairings are starlings. Males sing and wave their wings in order to attract a female. When she shows interest, he sings and waves his wings all the more, and then leads her to a likely place to nest. In the spring, you can often watch the starlings sing and display.

The grouse family includes great show-offs, like male capercaillies, black grouse, ruffed grouse, and prairie chickens. Males get together to display, using their colors, strangely shaped feathers, and odd noises. Females watch and choose the best-looking or most aggressive male. That way, their chicks should be strongest and most likely to survive.

Common gallinules fight for a mate and territory. Their noisy battles can often be seen in the spring. They kick with their feet and splash with their rounded wings.

Ruffs display, or "lek," at a group display ground, also called a "lek." Males have mock fights, and the strongest defend the center of the lek. Females creep up to see what's going on. They choose the most aggressive males to mate with. Male birds on the fringe sometimes get a chance to mate, too.

GRACEFUL PARTNERS

When grebes find a mate, they often stay together for life. But they go through elaborate displays every spring anyway, wagging their colorful head plumes in graceful "dances" on the water. The displays renew their bond, ensuring that both parents will be around during the many weeks of looking after the eggs and chicks.

Bald eagles and golden eagles display to their mates by showing off their skill in the air, swooping up and down in great roller coaster rides across the sky and diving at 100 miles an hour. These displays also warn other eagles "keep away—this piece of territory is mine."

Great crested grebes have elegant spring displays. They face each other and wag their heads, swim side by side and dive together, touch their backs with their beaks, and offer weeds to each other.

TROPICAL SPLENDOR

In the tropics, displays are taken to extremes. Birds of paradise have magnificent plumes that are used in courtship extravaganzas. Bowerbirds build elaborate structures and decorate them with colorful berries, leaves, and pieces of glass, wool, or plastic. Then they stand in the structure and display. The quetzals of the Central American forests have a long train of tail feathers that look like flying snakes when the males display in courtship flights.

The birds of paradise of New Guinea, such as this Raggiana bird of paradise, are famous for displaying their brilliant plumage.

If its song isn't enough to deter intruders, the European robin will fight to defend its territory. Some males even kill other robins in spring.

Male puffins fight over ownership of a nesting burrow. They grasp each other's bills and strike out with their feet, which have needle-sharp claws. Sometimes they roll down steep slopes and fall over cliffs.

DRUMMING AND BOOMING

Some birds use sound devices other than songs to establish territory or find a mate.

When snipe are claiming a territory in which to nest, they fly high in the air, spread out their stiff tail feathers, and dive steeply in a series of swoops. The tail feathers vibrate and make a loud humming noise with each dive. This is called drumming.

Another kind of drumming is used by woodpeckers. They find a hard branch that makes a loud, echoing sound when hit. Then they rain a stream of blows with their bill onto the wood, in a sudden, short, noisy burst of sound that carries through the forest.

Bitterns live in reeds so dense that they have a problem finding mates. They make their presence known with remarkably deep, booming sounds that carry more than a mile.

SONGS

In general, visual displays are more common in open habitats, whereas song is used to advertise a bird's presence where visibility is limited.

Bird songs and calls are used to convey messages. Songs that are used as a form of display while establishing a territory and attracting a mate are often the most beautiful. Some of the best songsters are the thrushes and warblers: if you can't identify any of the very similar-looking warblers by sight, try listening to their songs.

SONGFLIGHTS

Many small birds of open habitats fly up and sing over their territories, performing distinctive songflights. However, when they fly into the air, they are taking the risk of being seen more easily by predators.

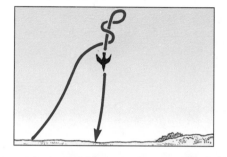

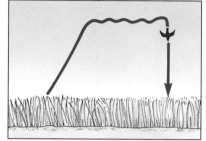

There are no perches in the open grasslands of North America where the bobolink lives. Instead the male flies up and hovers, starts his bubbling song, then descends in a quivering, fluttery flight, quite carried away with his own ecstatic singing.

Skylarks sing in high, hovering flights over open spaces where there are few perches from which to sing. They can keep up their continuous and excited song for half an hour or more. Afterward, they plummet to the ground and land silently.

Sedge warblers and whitethroats sing from bushes. Then every so often they fly up a short way in a steep, fluttery flight. They descend to another bush nearby, singing as they go. Reed warblers and lesser whitethroats never do this.

As the snipe dives, its stiff outer tail feathers tremble in the rush of air, making a loud humming noise.

Bitterns are heard but not seen—their booming calls carry more than a mile through the dense reeds where they live.

A VOICE IN THE AIR

Bird songs and calls are often beautiful, but some can get on your nerves. Whether or not they are attractive, songs are useful to the birdwatcher. Not only do they help you to find the bird more easily than by sight alone—you can hear a bird among dense trees where you may never see it—but they can usually help you to identify it, too.

THE SOUND OF BIRDS

Just as you need to learn what birds look like, you need to learn what they sound like too. The simplest way is to listen to common birds that you can see, and note the sounds they make: the *chirrup* call of a house sparrow or the bubbly song of a wren, for example. Many field guides describe some calls and songs. To learn less common songs and calls, listen to some familiar bird calls and compare them with the descriptions to find out how the author has interpreted the calls. The best way is to listen to professional recordings on cassettes.

If you want to hear bird songs among the sounds of tropical forests or remote lakes, the best recordings come on compact discs. The clarity and atmosphere are astonishing.

YOUR OWN RECORDINGS

Even with a small tape recorder and microphone, you can make good recordings of bird songs. Take a few cassette tapes and experiment. You can always tape over unsuccessful attempts. To avoid clicks on the recording, set the recorder to "record," with the "pause" button on, then release the "pause" button when you want to record.

Wind blowing on the microphone is often a problem. And you will be amazed how even a one-directional microphone picks up the noise of distant traffic, barking dogs, or people talking nearby. Be patient. It takes a lot of practice and experience to get results that compare with the professionals'.

One-directional, or "gun," microphones collect sound in a narrower beam than a general-purpose microphone. They can be mounted on a handle. The cover (shown detached) helps to filter out some of the background noise.

A good, sturdy cassette tape recorder is used by professionals to get high-quality recordings. If you are going to walk around with a recorder, use the shoulder strap to leave your hands free for holding the microphone and working the recorder. You can listen to the recordings on headphones as you go along.

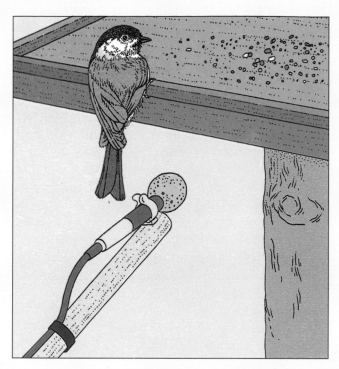

Try placing a microphone on a stand in a sheltered spot, perhaps near a bird feeder or a roost site. Use a long lead and sit in a blind or inside the house with your recorder. You can stay out of sight and not disturb the birds while you record their calls. You may be able to use headphones to hear what you are recording.

SONGS FOR THE RECORD

Each time you tape songs, record yourself giving the date, place, and time. On the cassette label, write the name of the bird, when and where you heard it, and what it was doing. A tape counter is useful. And with a tape-to-tape recorder, you can edit your tapes and keep only the best specimens.

REFLECTORS

The serious enthusiast may want to buy a parabolic reflector—a big, round dish, like a television satellite dish, with a microphone mounted in the center. The microphone collects sounds reflected from the dish, enabling you to record a magnified sound from a narrow source. You can focus on an individual bird and keep out many background noises, including other birds.

MAKING A PARABOLIC REFLECTOR

An old umbrella can be made into a parabolic reflector. A lining of aluminum foil or metallic silver paint will increase its reflecting properties. Make some test recordings with the microphone in different positions on the handle to find the focus of the sound. This will probably be about 6 to 8 inches from the top of the hood.

It is usually best to go out early. Birds, such as this male blackbird, sing best then, and there are fewer background noises. But don't just record the dawn chorus in the trees; winter flocks of geese, loons, and cranes also make spectacular sounds.

SPOTTER'S HINT
If you don't have a parabolic reflector, you can tape your microphone to a stick so that it doesn't pick up the rustling of your hands.

SURVIVAL OF THE YOUNG

In countries where people have good living conditions and modern medical care, each couple needs to have only two children for the population to remain stable. Most birds, however, die young. Birds must raise far more young so that the population as a whole does not dwindle away. For every two birds that survive to adulthood, the parents may have reared several dozen over the few years of their lives.

GAMBLING WITH DEATH

Birds are in constant danger. Many are killed by hawks and foxes. Others die of disease, starvation, and cold. Cars and pet cats kill large numbers of birds each year. Yet most species are stable—there are roughly the same number of each species year after year. This is because they maintain a balance with their environment. The number of eggs they lay and young they rear, and the number of young that survive to breeding age, exactly match the numbers needed to replace the adult birds as they die. If this balance were not maintained, the population would go up and down in a chaotic series of changes.

There are several ways in which the numbers are kept level. Every type of bird has its own way of rearing young, and each way works for the life that type leads. A lot depends on the food the parents can find. Feeding themselves is hard enough for a pair of adult birds. Having a family of growing chicks to feed is extra hard work. The parents will succeed only if their eggs hatch when there is an abundance of food.

Big birds such as golden and bald eagles have few enemies. They also live longer than small songbirds. They may have 10 years of life to rear just two young successfully. Eagles usually lay two eggs a year and rear only one chick. Even so, few chicks survive their first winter of fending for themselves. But eventually one or two will make it—just enough to keep the population going.

Wild geese, swans, and cranes feed in flocks in the winter, but family groups stay together within the larger gatherings. It is therefore easy to count how many pairs have reared young during the year and how many pairs have failed.

RAISING A BROOD

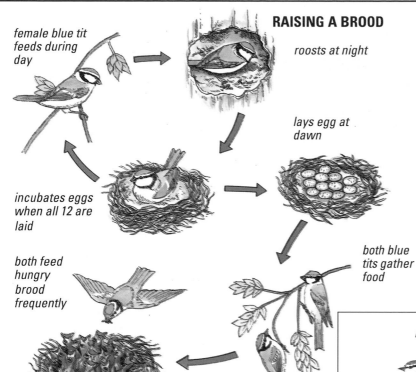

female blue tit feeds during day

roosts at night

lays egg at dawn

incubates eggs when all 12 are laid

both feed hungry brood frequently

both blue tits gather food

Blue tits really put all their eggs in one basket! They rear just one brood of young each year. The birds pair up, build a nest, and lay 10 to 12 eggs. They then incubate them (sit on them to keep them warm) until the eggs hatch at precisely the time when millions of tiny green caterpillars are hatching all over the fresh leaves of late spring. Suddenly, the blue tits can bring 800 caterpillars to their hungry chicks every day. A week too soon, or a week too late, and the food is not there. Only if they time it right can they feed a dozen chicks at once.

Blackbirds feed their chicks on worms. They can always get a few worms—but never hundreds at a time! They couldn't possibly find enough to feed 12 chicks at once, as blue tits do. Instead, they have four chicks at a time, but rear three families during the summer. In the end, although it has taken months, they rear as many chicks as the blue tits.

three clutches

spring   *summer*   *autumn*

A NATURAL BALANCE

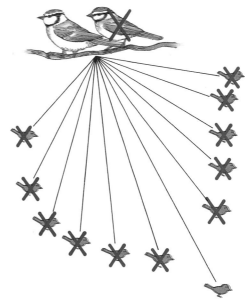

If 12 baby blue tits and both parents survived until next spring, there would be 14 birds where a year before there were two. But on average, 12 of the 14 birds die. If 11 were to die instead of 12, the blue tit population would increase by half: three birds would remain for every two. But large increases exhaust the local food supply, and many chicks would starve. Over time, the population stays about the same.

NESTS

Nests are not homes for adult birds. They are simply the places where birds lay their eggs.

Once the eggs are in the nest, parent birds incubate them. Many parents have bare "brood patches" on their bodies, where the feathers fall from a patch of skin so the eggs are next to the warm blood vessels. The eggs are kept at just the right temperature for the chicks to develop.

When the chick is old enough inside the egg, it may "talk" to its parent before it hatches. It uses a special "egg tooth" on the tip of its bill to break its way out of the hard shell. Some kinds of chicks may stay in the nest for a time; others leave right away.

EGGS

Eggs vary in color. Those laid in dark holes by owls, kingfishers, and woodpeckers are white, making them easier to see. Those laid on pebbly beaches, such as tern and plover eggs, are buff and spotted brown for perfect camouflage.

(not to scale)

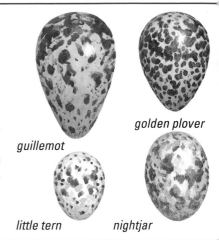

guillemot

golden plover

little tern

nightjar

EGGS

In many parts of the world, birds' eggs are protected by law. It is illegal to collect them, and it is a stupid thing to do. Eggs should be left to hatch into new young birds. Stealing very rare birds' eggs is particularly serious, as it can cause the species to become extinct.

Ravens make nests of large, heavy sticks placed under overhangs on sheer cliffs, well out of any predator's reach.

Woodpeckers dig their nests out of the trunks of trees, chipping out the wood with their chisel-like bills.

The reed warbler builds a nest in upright reeds. It fastens the deep cup-shaped nest to several growing reed stems.

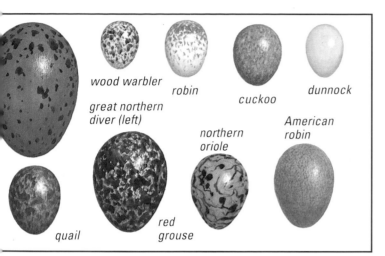

wood warbler

robin

cuckoo

dunnock

great northern
diver (left)

northern
oriole

American
robin

quail

red
grouse

JUVENILE AND IMMATURE

In bird books, young birds are often described by the terms "juvenile" and "immature." A juvenile bird is still in its first set of feathers, those it had when it left the nest. They have usually changed by autumn. An immature bird is not yet old enough to breed. With larger birds and seabirds, it may be three or four years or more before a bird has reached maturity.

LOST AND INJURED BIRDS

If you see a baby bird calling to be fed and you think it is lost, *leave it alone*. It almost certainly is not lost. When you go away its parents will come to feed it, so leave the area quickly. Never pick up a baby bird and take it home. Injured birds are extremely difficult to care for. If you find one, keep it warm in a well-ventilated box, then call for expert help from a local vet or the ASPCA. Most injured birds are likely to be put to sleep, as there is little we can do for them. Those that can recover will need constant care and attention.

Many species of cuckoo lay their eggs in the nests of other birds, such as this dunnock. The cuckoo watches other birds until she finds a nest with fresh eggs. Then she throws out one egg, lays one of her own, and leaves. The cuckoo egg hatches quickly and the baby cuckoo pushes out the other nestlings, so that it gets all the food from its foster parents.

YOUNG BIRDS

Helpless, naked, blind chicks need to be kept warm and sheltered. They take a long time to grow feathers and to grow large enough to leave the nest. This is typical of backyard birds and songbirds.

Baby ducklings are fluffy and active as soon as they hatch. They leave the nest and even feed themselves the day they are hatched. They may seem easy prey, but they can swim and dive, and they don't risk staying in a nest that might be sniffed out by a fox.

Owls start incubating as soon as the first egg is laid rather than waiting for the last egg. The chicks that hatch earlier get a head start and are able to grab more food. If there isn't enough food, the smaller chicks starve—but the others have a better chance to survive.

BEAKS AND FEET

A bird's beak, or bill, is comparable to both a hand and a tool. The bird grabs and handles food, combs feathers, and builds nests with its bill. Depending on the shape, a bill might swoop up prey, probe in the ground, or crack a nut. The bill fits the bird's way of life; by looking at the bill carefully, you can learn a lot about the bird. The feet also suit the bird's life and habitat. Both bills and feet give good clues when identifying birds.

BEAKS AND BILLS

Wading birds such as dowitchers, snipe, and godwits can probe with their long, slender bills in soft mud. The tip of the bill is sensitive enough to feel for worms. The bill is flexible enough to open up in the mud and close tight on a worm.

Birds of prey have hooked bills for tearing meat. Bald eagles rip open salmon; golden eagles tear away the hide of dead sheep and hares. A falcon's bill has a small notch behind the hook so the bird can break the neck of other birds or small mammals.

The spoonbill has a flattened bill that broadens into a disk at the tip. It holds the bill slightly open in shallow water and sweeps it from side to side. If it feels a fish, the bill snaps shut on it. Avocets do the same thing, but they eat tiny shrimps and worms in soft, wet mud or shallow water. Their bills are thin and curve upward.

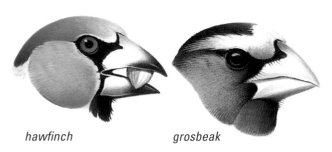

hawfinch　　　*grosbeak*

Hawfinch and grosbeak bills are designed for cracking hard seeds. Short, deep, triangular beaks have sharp cutting edges and powerful plates inside for crushing seeds. The cheeks bulge with strong muscles for working the bill around a cherry pit or a nut. These birds "peel" the seeds by rolling them with the tongue against the edge of the bill.

CRUSHING AND CATCHING

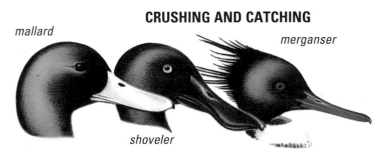

mallard　　　*merganser*

shoveler

Ducks have fascinating bills. Look at a mallard or shoveler on a park lake. Its bill is broad and flat. The inside surface is like a sieve and can filter tiny seeds from mud and water. Mergansers have long, narrow bills with tiny hooks and serrated edges like saws, for gripping strong, slippery fish.

The feet of bald eagles are powerful killing tools. They have strong muscles and long, curved claws with sharp points. The front claws hold the prey with a crushing grip, while the hind claw stabs it like a dagger.

LEGS AND TOES

Snipe have short legs but long toes, good for walking on mud, and long bills that probe the mud for food.

In contrast, stilts have long legs for walking in deep water and fairly short bills for picking insects from the water's surface.

A woodpecker's foot has two toes forward and two back (most birds have three forward, one back). The outer toe is long and can be swung sideways to grip a narrow branch.

The pipit has a long claw on its back toe, which helps it balance and walk through long grass. Most songbirds have short toes and claws and move in short hops.

nighthawk   nightjar

Swifts, nighthawks, and nightjars have tiny bills. But they all have huge mouths! They catch insects in flight in midair. Their mouths are wide and open up to snatch an insect, but the bill is almost useless. Nightjars have a line of stiff hairs around the mouth that helps guide in the insects.

SPOTTER'S HINT
When it has been raining or snowing, keep an eye out for footprints. You'll see where birds have been gathering, but it's difficult to identify which birds they were!

EATING TO SURVIVE

The main aim of most birds, most of the time, is to find food. Small birds, especially in the cold, short days of winter, or if they have young to care for, spend nearly all day searching. Watch flocks of tits, chickadees, and warblers and you will see them feeding nonstop. They can starve in a day without food. Larger birds can survive longer on fewer, bigger meals. Big birds of prey need only one meal a day and can go for several days without feeding if they have to. They spend more time resting and are not the all-action birds we sometimes imagine them to be. Gulls and ducks also spend many hours at rest.

FINDING FOOD

There are many ways of finding food. A lot depends on the kind of food, how much there is, and where it might be located. Some birds are loners because their food is never abundant, even though it may be widespread. For example, many thrushes eat worms or snails but there are rarely enough to feed whole flocks of birds at once. Each bird needs some space to move around in and search for scattered prey.

In contrast, seed-eaters, such as goldfinches and sparrows, can often find a lot of food in a small area. Therefore they can feed together and still find enough to go round. These birds live, feed, and even nest in larger groups.

LOOSE FLOCKS

Some birds, such as godwits on a beach, seem to be better at finding food if they are in a scattered, loose flock than if they are alone or in a dense flock. They find more worms and lose less to thieving gulls when they are in a group. But if there are too many in the group they begin to fight each other for food and the advantage is lost.

FINDING A NICHE

Some birds eat only one or two kinds of food. Others are less choosy. If two species compete for the same food, one often drives the other away. They can only live together if there is more than enough for both of them. If they eat different food, even two similar species may get along together, side by side. Some birds of prey live peacefully together in one area because they take

golden eagle 9 lb

hare 9 lb

buzzard 2 lb

rabbit 1 lb

sparrowhawk (female) (E) 9 oz

blackbird 3 oz

American kestrel (NA) 7 oz

beetle ⅕ oz

different prey. Hawks, such as sharp-shinned hawks and goshawks, eat birds, but avoid competition by taking different sizes of bird and by being different sizes themselves. This is true even between the sexes. Male sparrowhawks, for example, take sparrows and titmice. The larger females go for thrushes and pigeons.

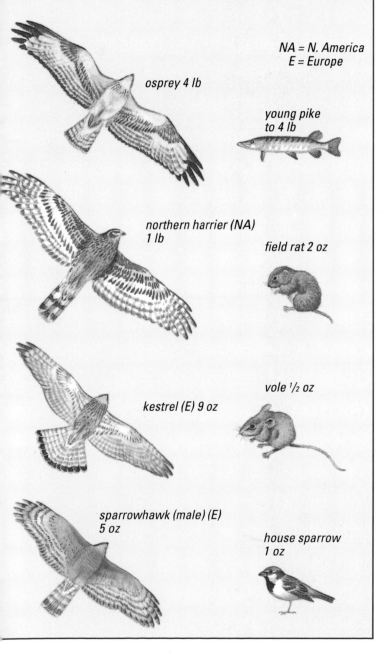

NA = N. America
E = Europe

osprey 4 lb

young pike to 4 lb

northern harrier (NA) 1 lb

field rat 2 oz

kestrel (E) 9 oz

vole ½ oz

sparrowhawk (male) (E) 5 oz

house sparrow 1 oz

SETTLING FOR LESS

The best feeding places for shorebirds, such as plovers, are open beaches with lots of food. Not all beaches are like this, though. Some may be uncovered only briefly at low tide. So the birds usually choose a site where there may be less food but it is available most of the day. If too many plovers choose the same site, they waste time squabbling, so they compromise further by spreading out.

Shrikes, such as this great gray shrike, catch large beetles, lizards, voles, and small birds by watching for them from a perch. They often spike their prey on a thorn to help tear them into pieces small enough to swallow.

FOOD PIRACY

Arctic skuas can catch fish but often find it is easier to wait for puffins, kittiwakes, and other birds to catch them instead. Then they chase and harass these birds until they drop the fish. The skuas will then snatch up the fish before it drops into the sea. They are typical food pirates. Skuas also eat small birds and mammals. The great skua, for example, preys on penguins' eggs and chicks.

THREATS TO THE FOOD SUPPLY

Some shorebirds migrate vast distances each year from southern Africa or South America to the Arctic. They must have guaranteed feeding sites along the way. River estuaries (where a river meets the sea) provide these vital sites. If people fill in and build on many more, the shorebirds may not find enough food. Red knots, for example, fly north across America and reach particular bays just when millions of horseshoe crabs come ashore to spawn. There are millions of crab eggs. The red knots have a feast, eating as much as they can, and there are still enough eggs to maintain the horseshoe crab population. If these bays were polluted or turned into an industrial site, the red knots would face disaster.

These shorebirds (red knots, with a few dunlins) rely on estuaries for most of their lives. Without these mud flats, which teem with millions of tiny creatures, they would not be able to feed during their globe-trotting travels or during the months when they are away from the Arctic.

STAYING PUT OR MOVING ON

Some owls stay in one small area all their lives; others move around to find the best hunting. Tawny owls and great horned owls stay in one place and learn every inch of it. They can find enough to eat even in bad years when food is scarce because they know the best places to find prey. Long-eared and snowy owls do not need to know their territories well because they move on when food is scarce and find a better hunting ground.

OWL PELLETS

If you can find a place where an owl or other bird of prey roosts, you can collect some pellets—the pieces of prey that can't be digested and are coughed back up through the mouth. If you ease them apart in a dish or a pan of water, you can pick out bones, feathers, beetles' wings, and so on. You can see just what the bird has had for dinner!

Use tweezers to clean the bones and teeth you find. Zoology textbooks might help you to identify the parts.

WAYS OF FEEDING

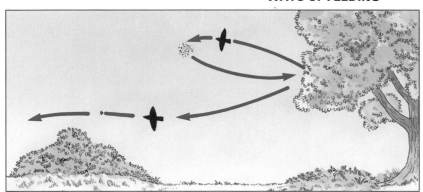

Flycatchers swoop out from a perch to snatch flies in midair. For this reason they prefer clearings or woodland edges to dense trees. Can you observe whether they are catching insects that fly over sunny spaces and show up against a dark background?

Great titmice feed on and around big branches, blue titmice hop onto smaller twigs, and tiny coal titmice move to the tips of the thinnest sprigs. These birds feed in a mixed flock but don't compete for the same food.

SPOTTER'S HINT
Early spring migrants that rely on insects for food find them few and far between. You often see these birds beside lakes and ponds, where swarms of tiny flies hatch early.

The slender, pointed bill of the goldfinch is made for picking seeds from deep inside thistles and teasels.

Shelducks find a good nest burrow and defend a territory around it, keeping other shelducks away. Then the male goes off to find a good feeding territory on the beach and stakes a claim to that, too. When the chicks hatch, they are led from the nest across the dunes to the beach, where their feeding area has already been reserved.

51

FLOCKS

Some birds are never seen more than a few at a time —perhaps a family group at most—while others form large gatherings known as flocks. There are several reasons for flocking, and also for staying in ones and twos. If a bird feeds on food that is found in small quantities over a large area, there is only enough food in one place for one or two birds at a time. But where food is plentiful, there is no reason why hundreds of birds should not feed together.

Spectacular flocks of oystercatchers flash black and white as they take off. Dazzled predators, such as peregrines, find it difficult to concentrate on one bird and may miss them all!

SAFETY IN NUMBERS

A bird on its own might escape being seen by a predator. But if it is seen, the predator has a good chance of catching it. Birds in a flock are more likely to spot a predator—many eyes are better than two— and if the predator comes close, there's a good chance it will kill one of the others! So when foxes or hawks are around, most birds in open spaces are safer in flocks than if they scatter.

FINDING FOOD

Flocks can also make it easier to find food. A bird on its own cannot search very quickly, but in a flock one of the birds is sure to find something—then all the rest can join in.

Shorebirds on a muddy estuary may feed in dense flocks and find food more efficiently than if they were widely spaced. They can spend more time eating and less time watching out for hawks. On the other hand, birds that eat worms feed more effectively on their own because worms wriggle down into the mud when disturbed by the noise of too many pattering feet. But even these birds form flocks when the tide comes in and move upshore to rest in a sheltered, safe place.

Cattle egrets feed in small groups in fields and drier marshland, often alongside cattle. They flock together to roost, as safe places are few.

EVENING ROOSTS

Even birds that feed in small groups may form larger flocks to spend the night. This may be because they need a safe place to sleep, like gulls on a lake or starlings in the reeds, but it also helps those that have found little food to follow better-fed birds to good feeding areas the next morning. In roosting flocks the older, stronger birds sleep in the center, where it is warm and safest from predators, leaving younger and weaker birds out in the cold.

WATCHING FLOCKS

Look for flocks and note down the numbers of birds you see. Are the flocks of one species, two, or more? Some shorebirds and ducks stay separate, others intermingle. Starling flocks are exclusive, but thrush flocks can be made up of two or three species together.

It is interesting to study the behavior of the flock as a whole rather than one bird at a time. For example, do winter plover flocks select the same fields year after year? Do they go for the same crops? Are they feeding in open spaces, or close to hedges and trees? Do gulls steal the plovers' food? If so, do the less experienced young plovers lose more food to the gulls than adults?

Small flocks can be easily counted one by one. But bigger groups need a quicker method: Count 10 birds, then divide the flock into tens, or hundreds, and add up the groups.

Flocks of black-headed gulls follow the farm plow because huge numbers of worms and grubs are turned up—there's plenty of food for all.

ON THE LOOKOUT

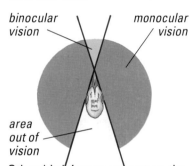

binocular vision   monocular vision

area out of vision

Birds of prey have magnificent eyesight. They see things in better detail than we do. Like us, they have binocular vision: Their eyes face forward, so they can focus on their prey and judge distance well.

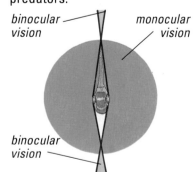

binocular vision   monocular vision

area out of vision

Other birds' eyes are set on the sides of their heads. This gives them less binocular vision but a wider field of view for spotting predators.

binocular vision   monocular vision

binocular vision

The woodcock's eyes are placed so that it can see completely around and behind its own head.

MIGRATION

Birds can fly vast distances and even cross the greatest oceans. Many of them migrate: They live in one part of the world for one season of the year, and move elsewhere for another season. They migrate to avoid bad winter weather, or to find new supplies of food or reach remote breeding grounds.

Many birds, such as warblers and swallows, find the warm northern summers, with long, hot days and abundant insects, an irresistible attraction. Warblers fatten up before they leave in autumn on their long nonstop flights. Most migrate at night, navigating by the moon and stars. Swallows migrate by day, using the sun as a guide and eating insects as they go.

When the warblers and swallows fly off for the winter, other birds—thrushes, waxwings, woodpeckers, owls and other birds of prey—move into the area they have left. They come from farther north, or they escape the cold winters in the middle of northern continents by flying to the milder coastal regions.

NORTHERN VISITORS

Many shorebirds breed on northern tundra (treeless plains), where the summer is short, but daylight lasts almost 24 hours. By autumn it is cold and dark and the birds fly south. They return in late spring, after the snow begins to melt.

A DANGEROUS JOURNEY

Migration is difficult because birds face great danger crossing mountains, seas, and deserts; small birds become exhausted. Lighthouse beams and lights on oil rigs at sea confuse migrating birds, and many dash themselves to death against the dazzling lights.

Birds are carefully trapped by scientists who put bands on their legs. If a bird is later found dead or is trapped again, the tiny label shows where it has come from and how long it has lived.

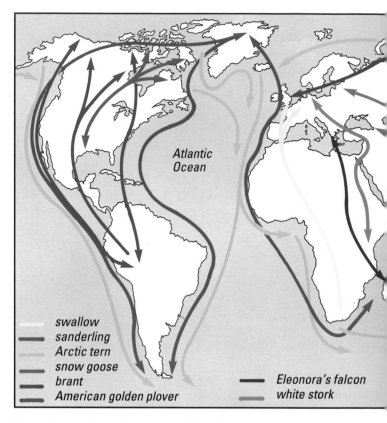

Atlantic Ocean

swallow
sanderling
Arctic tern
snow goose
brant
American golden plover
Eleonora's falcon
white stork

Migrating swallows fly south to Africa. Sanderlings and Arctic terns fly right across the globe; brant and snow geese stay in the Northern Hemisphere. American golden plovers are among the fastest migrants; white storks take lots of time

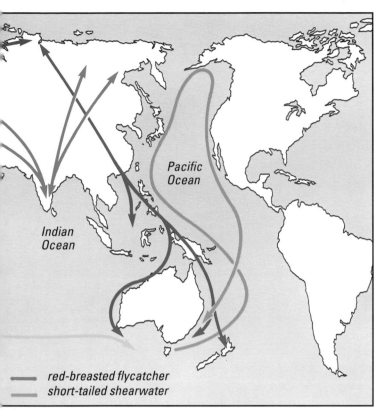

red-breasted flycatcher
short-tailed shearwater

soaring from Europe to Africa. Eleonora's falcons eat smaller migrants along their route. Short-tailed shearwaters travel the oceans worldwide. Red-breasted flycatchers fly to India from all across Asia.

Waxwings and cedar waxwings eat insects when they are plentiful in summer, but turn to fleshy berries in winter. They eat more than their own body weight each day, and need plenty of water, too.

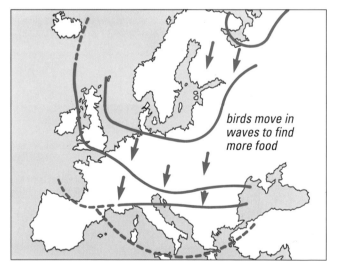

birds move in waves to find more food

Shorebirds need to feed in rich estuary mud. Not many estuaries are suitable; the best act as migration "service stations" for millions of birds on their globe-trotting travels. Without the estuaries—many of which are under threat from urban and industrial development—the birds would die.

If birds such as waxwings have had two or three successful breeding seasons, their numbers will be high. If the berry crop is then poor, large flocks of birds will fly great distances in search of new sources of food. This is called an "irruption" from their normal range.

55

SPRING MIGRATION

Migration time is exciting for the birdwatcher. In spring, birds are eager to get to their breeding areas and claim a territory. Once the weather is good, they move quickly. If you want to see migrating loons or terns at a local lake, you will have to go as often as possible because they will not be there for long. A migrant may pause for only an hour or so to rest and feed before continuing on its way.

Excited by the prospect of good birdwatching, people gather at special migration watch points to see the show. Migrating hawks at Hawk Mountain, Pennsylvania, storks at Gibraltar, and incoming migrants along the coast of the English Channel all attract enthusiasts in autumn.

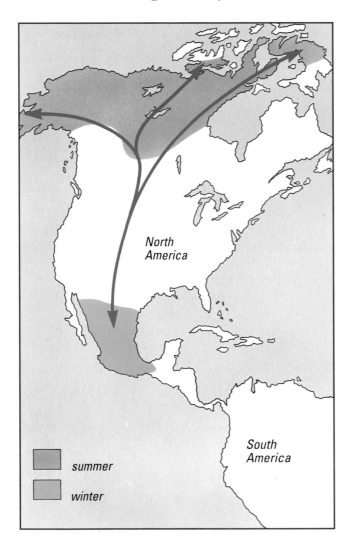

North America

South America

☐ summer

☐ winter

North American cranes are protected in their nesting areas and also where they spend the winter. But they need safe, undisturbed places during their long migration flights, too. The riverbeds where sandhill cranes have paused during their flights over thousands of years are being turned into farmland, and the cranes are finding it more and more difficult to feed and rest on their long journeys.

Sandhill cranes are among the most spectacular of migrating birds. Thousands fly south each autumn from Alaska and northern Canada to the southern United States and Mexico. Their trumpeting calls can be heard a mile away. Sometimes flocks fly so high overhead that they can be heard from the ground but not seen.

White storks gather in great flocks at narrow sea crossings. They need to fly over warm land to glide on rising air currents; they cannot fly far over water. Every autumn at places such as Gibraltar and the Bosporus, storks from all over Europe gather before crossing over to Africa.

OFF-COURSE RARITIES

Caught up in the excitement of spring migration, some birds fly too far. Instead of stopping at the right place, they "overshoot." This means there are sometimes odd birds to be seen: The reddish egret, of southeastern Texas, was recently seen in Jamaica Bay, Queens—the first New York State sighting.

In autumn, things are more relaxed. Many birds stop to rest and feed in the same spot for days or weeks, and there is less urgency about their journey. But the young birds hatched that summer face their first long-distance flights in autumn. They often get lost, drift off course, or start out in the wrong direction.

REVERSE MIGRATION

Reverse migration is one theory why rare birds such as Russian warblers turn up in strange places. They set off along the right route but in the wrong direction, and reach western Europe instead of southeast Asia! These lost strays make autumn even better than spring for seeing rare birds off course. But don't expect to find many such rarities. Most are a once-in-a-lifetime chance.

Small warblers that are thousands of miles off course, such as this desert warbler, are a rare sight in Europe. They shouldn't be there at all!

Few rarities are as spectacular as the bee-eater. Common in southern Europe, it turns up in northern France and England only by accident, having flown too far north on its migration from Africa.

DIVING FOR A LIVING

Many birds are brilliant divers. Some, such as grebes and loons, swim along the surface and then sink, disappearing without a trace. Others, such as coots, go under with a head-first dive, leaping forward and rolling under with a splash. Some birds dive from a perch—kingfishers wait until they see a fish, then plunge headlong from an overhanging branch or jetty. Kingfishers and some other birds can also dive from the air. The best are the terns, gannets, and brown pelicans. They fly over the water, looking down for fish, then plunge in after it with a loud splash.

All these birds are after fish or other water creatures. A few other birds, such as gadwalls, hang around diving coots and grebes to pick up scraps from the weeds they bring to the surface.

A trip to the sea is a good chance to watch some of these diving birds.

Not all kingfishers (left) dive into water. African brown-hooded kingfishers dive from tree perches to catch insects in midair.

The dipper (left) is an unusual songbird that dives and even walks underwater. Dippers don't have webbed feet and look nothing like ducks. They are round and dumpy, but they live in fast streams and have big, strong feet that grip the bottom. They face into the current, leaning forward and slightly opening their wings so the force of the water pushes them down. They move about looking for caddisfly larvae and other water grubs.

common tern

brown pelican

guillemot

common loon

shearwater

cormorant

SPECIAL ADAPTATIONS

Some diving birds are specially equipped for the job. Gannets dive from 100 feet or more and hit the water with a terrific smack that would hurt you or me! But they have cushions of air under the skin of the head and neck. The bones at the base of the bill are soft and spongy. Their eyes are shielded by a tough membrane, and their nostrils close to keep out the water. And they have dense feathers all over their bodies. They are made for hitting the water hard without being knocked out.

UNDERWATER SWIMMERS

Many birds are designed for swimming underwater. They often have webbed feet or lobed toes. On the strong push backward, the toes are spread apart and the broad webs shove the water like oars. On the forward stroke, the toes are closed and the webs fold up to give the least resistance.

Other birds swim with their wings instead of their feet. Guillemots (pronounced GILL-uh-mots) can be watched under clear water from the top of their nesting cliffs. They use their wings somewhat like seals use their flippers. Another seabird, the puffin, "flies" better under water than in the air, swimming with its wings. In the air, its wings are so small that it flies with a continuous, rapid whir.

DIVING BIRDS

You can make an interesting project by timing the dives of the various ducks, grebes, and coots at different ponds and lakes. Coots go under and come up in the same spot. If you have an idea of the water depth, time their dives and see whether they dive longer in deeper water. Do they bring food to the surface or swallow it under water? Grebes, mergansers, and goldeneyes can move long distances under water and come up far from where you saw them first dive under—so watch carefully!

3 feet = 5 seconds

6 feet = 10 seconds

9 feet = 15 seconds

NIGHT BIRDS

Few of us go out in really black, deep night. Most of our nights are softened by street lights or the glow from distant cities. Therefore it is not easy to know what night is really like for night birds far from our homes. On the other hand, many night birds now have to put up with our lights, too.

NIGHTS AT SEA

Shearwaters and petrels are excellent fliers and swimmers, but they are so clumsy on land that in the light they are easy prey for big gulls. They come to their nesting burrows only in the dark—even a bright moon will put them off—and find their way by their sense of smell and by listening for the call of their mate on the nest. In large colonies—often thousands—it is amazing that any shearwater can recognize its mate's call in the hubbub.

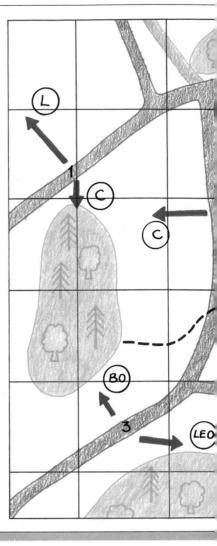

BIRDS AT NIGHT
Oak Cottage Vale, Friday 12 June 1992, 9.30pm. There was a full moon, and no cloud. Light wind from east.

1. At dusk, lapwings seen and heard in distance NW. Loud cuckoo in woods to S. Stayed 15 minutes.

2. Same cuckoo as at 1? calling continuously. Noisy call and flapping wings of disturbed pheasant N. Noisy mallards(?) flying over SE – probably flying to lake. Aircraft flew over. Stayed 20 minutes.

3. First barn owl of year called twice NW. Dad thinks he heard long-eared owl SE, only one call in distance. Stayed 15 minutes.

Home at 10.30pm.

You can "birdwatch" at night by listening to songs and calls. Go with other birders to a familiar area of woodland or shore that is far from lights and noisy traffic. Bring a local map with you, and mark on it what you hear and where. Always go with an experienced leader. It's sometimes wise to let the police know where you'll be.

Black skimmers feed by dragging the long tip of their lower bill through water, ready to snap up fish. At night they make a trail through phosphorescent plankton, which glow when disturbed. This glow attracts fish, and the skimmer goes back over its own track to catch them.

North

ACTIVITY AT NIGHT

LIGHT	TWILIGHT	DARK

Grasshopper warblers sing on moist, warm summer evenings

At dusk, the hobby, a falcon, catches moths; in autumn, it will chase swallows

Geese fly to roost, but may keep on feeding on a moonlit night

Mallards sometimes feed after dark to avoid people

Lapwings are still active into twilight, often calling at night

A barn owl will hunt early if it has a family to feed

Short-eared owls hunt in the evening after their prey, the northern harrier, has gone to roost

Gallinules can be heard flying overhead at night, looking for new ponds

The nightjar comes out just after sunset, when moths are most active

The kestrel often hunts at dusk, the peak of vole activity

Cuckoos sing until dark in early summer

Screech owls wait for true darkness

The large-eyed stone curlew begins to call at twilight and flies off to good feeding areas

Woodcocks hunt for worms at night

The noisy oystercatcher's piping call can be heard beside northern coasts very late at night

NIGHT SIGHT

Can an owl see in pitch dark? Not really. It can see slightly better than we can in dim light and its eyes are better than ours at seeing details in the dark. Owls move around at night by knowing their home areas inside out, by picking out what details they can, and by using their sensitive ears, which are shaped and positioned for pinpointing small sounds. Because the left and right ears of owls are different sizes (and one is often higher on the head than the other), they pick up sounds slightly differently, giving a 3-D effect to sound, comparable to what we see with our eyes. Some owls can hear a mouse squeak under a snowdrift and dive at the sound.

Owls have fringes along their feathers, like fine hair. The fringes deaden the noise their wings make, so they are silent in flight. They can hear their prey moving, but the prey can't hear them coming.

BIRDS OF PREY

Exciting to watch, birds of prey are much misunderstood. Some are killers, at the top of the food chain. They are predators, like lions and wolves, usually killing the weaker members of the species on which they prey. But they rarely significantly reduce the numbers of their prey; it is usually the availability of prey that controls the predators. For example, if there is a population increase of mice and voles, there will be a similar increase of kestrels and owls to eat them. However, if the kestrels and owls reduce the numbers of prey too drastically, they themselves begin to starve and decline in numbers. So over time, predator and prey tend to reach a balance.

CARRION EATERS

Many birds of prey, such as vultures and condors, are scavengers who eat carrion—animals that are already dead. This may seem nasty, but they do a useful job by clearing away dead carcasses. Most carrion eaters have long beaks and necks to probe among the carcasses. Eagles eat carrion too.

The sharp claws of a kestrel are perfect for catching voles and beetles. If necessary, the bill is used to kill the captured prey.

BIRD HUNTERS

Some falcons (such as the merlin and peregrine) and hawks (such as the goshawk) are bird hunters. They fly fast and are thrilling to see. Goshawks live in the northern forests of North America, Europe, and Asia. They keep out of sight, then ambush smaller birds. To see one, you need to sit quietly by a forest clearing and wait patiently.

Small falcons, such as kestrels, eat voles and beetles. Buzzards prefer rabbits but will eat worms when necessary.

Black vultures look for scraps or dead animals as they fly. If one spots food and descends, others follow it down. Soon large flocks gather as if from nowhere.

NIGHT HUNTERS

At night, another specialized bird of prey takes over—the owl. Many owls survive only by knowing every last detail of their territories and by having exclusive hunting rights there. If there are no other owls around, they can move easily in the dark and find enough food. This is why owls spend so much time doing the rounds and "singing" with their strange hooting calls. They are telling other owls, "This patch is occupied."

HOW THEY HUNT

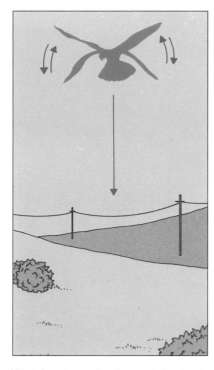

In the vast open wilderness where it hunts, the golden eagle has a good view but needs to dive fast to get close to its prey. It catches hares or grouse after a low, rapid chase close to the ground or a steeper dive from high in the sky.

Watch a hovering kestrel. Its body may move in the breeze, but its head is very still while it watches the ground below. If it spots something, it dives, perhaps pausing to check again halfway down.

A pigeon might escape a peregrine falcon in level flight. But the peregrine soars above its prey and drops in a lightning-fast dive, striking with its claws. Few birds can escape it.

HUNTING GROUNDS

The commonest birds of prey are the ones that eat the more numerous rodents and insects. Because the large eagles, hawks, and falcons prey on other birds and mammals and need large and undisturbed hunting territories, they are always rare. There isn't enough food for them to be common.

POISON: A DEADLY BUSINESS

Crows and foxes, which can slaughter huge numbers of game birds and chickens, are detested by many hunters and farmers. Although it is illegal, poison is often put out to kill them, using a dead rabbit or chicken as bait. Frequently, birds of prey, some from endangered species, eat this bait and die.

BIRDS OF THE OCEAN

One of the most remarkable things about ocean birds is that they come back year after year to the same island or coastal cliff to nest. Imagine a tiny petrel—no bigger than a starling—flying low over the ocean waves for months on end. It may have traveled thousands of miles. All it can see is the sky and a few acres of ocean below. Yet each spring it not only finds the island where it nests, but even goes ashore at night and finds the very same burrow! Nobody can explain how it is done.

STAYING ALOFT

Incredibly, some ocean birds don't swim! Frigatebirds and sooty terns stay off the water because their feathers, not rich enough in oils, would become waterlogged and they might sink. Instead, they fly thousands of miles across the oceans, soaring and gliding on the wind, never settling for an instant. They feed on fish at the water's surface and on flying fish, snatching them up in their bills.

You can see surprising numbers of birds from an ordinary ferry. Find a sheltered spot where the deck doesn't vibrate too much. Keep scanning the sea with your binoculars. Don't look too far away from the ship—most birds are quite small! Sometimes a flock of gulls or terns will follow the ship.

TRACKING THE ALBATROSS

Albatrosses have been caught and fitted with tiny transmitters, then followed by satellite: They can travel 600 miles a day, day after day. Because they glide on the air currents that sweep up over big waves, they can live only in windy parts of the world. They are the ultimate ocean travelers.

GLIDING ON THE WIND

Wherever air rises, birds can stay airborne using very little energy. A wind off the sea rises above a cliff, and gulls and fulmars can soar gracefully on its currents.

If a wind blows off the land, it falls over the cliff edge. However, the many swirling eddies create updrafts which birds use to glide above the waves and stay near land.

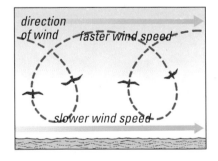

Simply by dragging across the waves, air is slowed down at the sea's surface. Shearwaters rise to the faster air above, to gain speed for their long glides downward.

Rows of whirring guillemots, screaming kittiwakes, wheeling gulls—coastal cliffs, like this one on the North Pacific coast, have thriving bird life unlike anywhere else.

Unlike other wading birds, gray phalaropes often feed while sitting on the water. They snatch up floating insects and tiny passing fish. Their nesting grounds are in the far north, mostly on the tundra, where insects are abundant. In winter they spend months at sea. It seems a hard life for such delicate-looking birds.

LANDING TO NEST

All ocean birds must come on land to nest. Most form large colonies on rocky cliffs or islands; tropical fairy terns, frigatebirds, and a few others gather in trees. Because young albatrosses can take 10 months to grow flight feathers, albatrosses often rear only one chick every two years. The small shearwaters and petrels also have long breeding seasons; their eggs take many weeks to hatch and their chicks months to fly. Ocean birds are also slow to reach breeding condition; albatrosses may not begin to breed until they are 10 to 15 years old. Because a large portion of the population is made up of immature birds scattered over the seas, if a disaster wipes out a breeding colony there are always enough birds at sea to replace them—provided suitable nesting grounds remain.

tufted puffin

rhinoceros auklet

kittiwake

guillemot

pigeon guillemot

ancient murrelet

pelagic cormorant

Brandt's cormorant

western gull

black turnstone

black oystercatcher

BIRDS IN THE WOODS

The forest provides a home not only for some of the most common and familiar birds but for rarer birds, too. What birds you see in the woods depends on the kinds of trees growing there. Some birds can be found in almost any kind of tree; others are more selective. To find your bird, learn its tree.

THE WONDERFUL OAK

The various oak trees of America and Europe are home to many kinds of insects. Beetles lay eggs under the bark, grubs tunnel in the wood, caterpillars eat the leaves, wasp larvae make galls. With so much to eat, many birds prefer oaks to all other trees. They are gnarled and rough, so they also provide plenty of places to nest. But specialists seek out other trees. For example, beech trees produce masses of small nuts, called beechnuts, which are enclosed in prickly burs. Chaffinches and great tits love them. Crossbills have beaks made for prying seeds out of cones, and they prefer spruce, pine, and larch.

The red-headed woodpecker of North America stores acorns and seeds under bark, to be eaten in times of shortage.

Woodland birds are specialized for life in a rich habitat. Boring for grubs in the wood, cracking nuts, picking fruits, catching insects—all require different skills.

Sapsuckers, a group of North American woodpeckers, bore holes in bark and eat the dripping sap and the insects attracted to it.

SIGNS OF FEEDING

It may be possible to detect the presence of birds even when they are nowhere to be seen. They leave behind signs of what they were eating. Split seeds, emptied nut cases, fallen pine cones, even holes probed into mud or chipped into fallen logs, all give us useful clues.

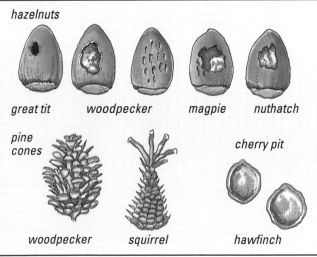

hazelnuts

great tit   woodpecker   magpie   nuthatch

pine cones

woodpecker   squirrel

cherry pit

hawfinch

Nuthatches leave several telltale signs. Nuts and berries wedged into crevices in tree bark, where they can be pecked at more easily, are typical nuthatch work.

The flicker is a woodpecker, and like the green woodpecker in Europe (below), it often eats ants.

The green woodpecker has a long tongue coiled around its skull. The bird pushes its tongue into ant hills and catches ants with the tip.

The brown creeper is difficult to spot on tree bark because of its streaked brown plumage.

To cover the biggest area of bark with the least effort, creepers start at the bottom of each tree and spiral upward.

HABITAT VARIATION

It isn't just food that affects a bird's choice of habitat. Pied flycatchers catch insects at the base of trees, so they prefer open woods where grazing animals keep down the undergrowth. Wood warblers nest in open spaces under trees; they like tall beeches with broad leaves that block the light so that nothing grows below. Many birds live at the woodland edge, where they find food in the open and safety among the trees and shrubs. Many birds nest in holes, so you won't find them in stands of conifers, which don't have holes. You can see more birds around ragged edges and alongside clearings than in deep forests or along straight, wide roads.

PATIENT TRACKING

Woodland birds are hard to see when trees are in leaf; the woods may even seem empty. You'll probably hear birds first; then you can track them down. You see more at a pool where birds come to drink, so sit quietly out of sight. In autumn, walk around until you find a mixed bird flock, then try to stick with it.

THE DAWN CHORUS

Most brilliant singers are birds of the woods. In North America, the hermit thrush and wood thrush are star performers. Go to the woods early on a spring or summer morning to hear all the forest birds sing loudly at daybreak, in a marvelous dawn chorus that you will never forget. Most birds will make themselves scarce when you arrive, but sit still and wait, and they will begin to move about and sing again.

Later in the year you will hear the young birds calling to be fed. They scatter through the trees and hide among the leaves. Once their chicks are able to fly, some birds, such as pied flycatchers, just seem to disappear.

LAKES AND RIVERS

All birds need water to drink, but some are specially equipped to spend all their lives on or alongside water. Obvious water birds are ducks and swans. Less well known are the grebes and loons and even some small birds such as kingfishers.

DIVING DUCKS

The two main groups of freshwater ducks are those that dive for food and those that find it by dabbling among the plants and grasses. Diving ducks feed on underwater plants, water snails, or fish.

In winter, water birds often separate into smaller flocks, reducing competition for food. In many species of diving ducks the males are bigger and stronger than the females and fly farther in their search for food. The flocks become divided into mostly female and mostly male groups, which helps them survive because it allows them to hunt over a wider range. Other kinds of birds also tend to form separate male flocks in winter. The chaffinch, a European songbird, bears the scientific name *Fringilla coelebs*, meaning "bachelor bird," for this reason.

Exotic ducks, such as this brightly colored male mandarin, from Asia, often turn out to have escaped from zoos and wildlife parks.

WATERSIDE WATCH

Spring and autumn days beside a freshwater lake can be exciting. This is a good time to watch for migrants dropping in to feed for an hour or even a day or two. Many of the rarest finds are shorebirds stopping beside reservoirs or along the muddy edges of coastal pools.

Be careful when watching waterside birds. If you go slowly and quietly to the water's edge and then sit still, you are less likely to scare away shy birds.

Look in both directions as you approach, listening for bird calls. Try not to stand up on banks or walls so that you are silhouetted against the sky. You may find wagtails, pipits, and shorebirds alongside the concrete slope of a reservoir

Look along the muddy shoreline for teal, snipe, and sandpipers. Quickly check the water, too: Shy birds such as teal might be flying off, while coots, grebes, and cormorants will be diving under water.

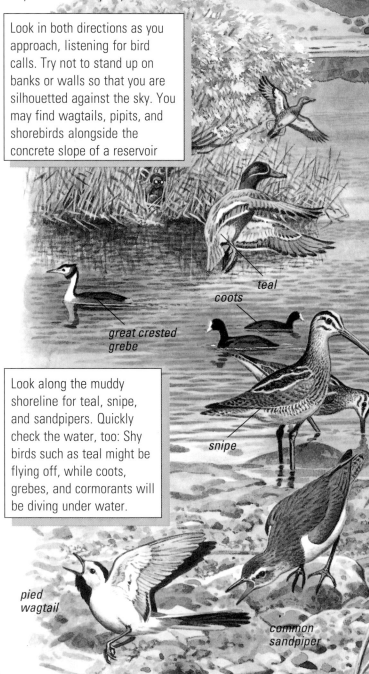

teal

coots

great crested grebe

snipe

pied wagtail

common sandpiper

black-headed gulls

You will see many kinds of gulls, and perhaps also terns, over the water. Black terns catch insects from the surface; common terns plunge in for fish.

black terns

heron

sedge warbler

kingfisher

In the reeds you might spot a kingfisher or a heron. Listen and watch for warblers in summer. In autumn, swallows and wagtails roost in waterside reeds. Huge flocks of starlings sometimes dive into the reeds to spend the night in safety.

reed warbler

DABBLING DUCKS

Dabbling ducks feed on plants or seeds that are found on or just below the surface of the water or mud. They lower their bills to the water while tilting up, or upending, their backsides, and filter food with rapid splashing movements of their sieve-like bills. The dabblers include the mallard, gadwall, and shoveler. Some, such as the wigeon, are also grazers, nibbling grasses along the shore.

With its broadly lobed toes, the coot can walk on land, pecking at grass; swim on the surface; or dive under water to reach nutritious water weeds.

GREBES AND COOTS

Grebes have short legs placed far back on the body, perfect for swimming but useless for walking. Grebes do not have flattened bills, like ducks, but dagger-like bills like those of herons. Their feet are not webbed but have broad, flattened lobes along each toe. They eat fish which they catch under water. Coots, too, have lobed toes; they swim and dive, but eat weeds and come out to crop the grass on dry land. They are neither ducks nor grebes but look a little like them. Coots are related to rails, which creep about secretively in waterside vegetation and swamps.

WHERE THE RIVER MEETS THE SEA

A winding river with stands of reeds and willow thickets is a lovely place for a walk. Unfortunately, fewer rivers are now accessible. Their banks have been cleared and lawns planted, which makes them less varied and interesting to birds.

If you want to see lots of birds, go to where two different habitats meet. At this estuary on the Atlantic Coast, you have the best of all worlds: land and sea, plus the shoreline itself.

ESTUARIES

It can be fascinating to walk down a river to its estuary, where it broadens as it flows into the sea. There, the fresh, often muddy, water meets the salt sea, and twice-daily tides move salt water in and out along the river channel. It seems a difficult place to live, but many birds don't mind the constant changes.

Watch for ducks here. Some, such as mallards, live anywhere near water. Mergansers nest by the river but fly out to sea. Scoters and eiders will be beyond the river mouth in the bay; they rarely come onto the fresh water.

Shorebirds increase as you approach the sea. The riverside is good for belted kingfishers. By the river mouth there will be more oystercatchers, dunlins, and sanderlings.

kestrel

boat-tailed grackles

oystercatchers

osprey

bank swallows

eastern meadowlark

SALT MARSHES

Salt marshes by river mouths are great places for birds. Gulls often nest in big colonies on the marsh. In wintertime, huge flocks of ducks, geese, and shorebirds feed in the muddy creeks and rest on the marsh at high tide.

ON THE SHORE

In summer, look for common terns. They fish along some rivers but mostly prefer the sea. They nest along the shore. If you get too close to their nest area, terns will become agitated and fly noisily around your head until you move off. Go quickly, because while they are driving you away, crows and gulls could be getting at their eggs.

CHOOSE YOUR PATH

Always be with a local guide on your birdwatching walks near estuaries. Use a good map if you walk along a river. It is easy to get cut off by a creek and have to walk a long way back to find a way around. Be especially careful as you near an estuary. Tides race in very fast and can cut you off on mudbanks or salt marshes. High tides can be deadly. Make sure you know the times of the tides, and don't go where you might have trouble getting back when the water rises.

VACATION DIARY

If you go on a seaside vacation, keep a bird diary. Take color photographs of the beach and the estuary and put them in your book. Include pictures of friends and family, too —you will enjoy looking at them in years to come.

As well as writing down all the birds you see, note which are on the river, which are on the sea, and which are in between. Jot down all your most interesting memories of the occasion and the birds you saw. For example, if you had a fantastic view of a special bird at close range, in brilliant sunlight, say so. It will help bring back memories of your sightings when you read your diaries later.

Make a map of the estuary, showing the high-water and low-water levels, the areas of sand, mud, pebbles, and marsh, and your regular walking routes. Add details, such as the direction of the sun and wind. Mark your bird sightings on the map.

gulls and terns

Common merganser

common eiders

scaup

black scoters

song sparrow

sanderlings

willets

HIGH IN THE MOUNTAINS

Birds that roost on high mountain peaks are not easy for most birdwatchers to study, but they are exciting. If you can join a hike up a mountain trail, perhaps you will see a variety of birds along the way.

UPLAND BIRDS

Many birds live on high meadows and slopes below the stark mountain peaks. These birds may be difficult to spot because there are few of them spread over vast areas. They are hard to get close to. You need to be at your best to stalk them, and some you will be able to see only from a distance with a telescope.

BIG BIRDS OF PREY

Mountain birds include the spectacular golden eagle. It often circles the highest peaks, going around in broad, slow arcs without beating its wings. Don't mistake buzzards for eagles. Buzzards are frequently lower down, and you can get much closer to them. You can rarely get close to an eagle.

BREEDING LOWLAND BIRDS

Many birds that spend the winter on lowland fields or estuaries go upland to nest. In North America, the mountain plover is not a bird of mountain peaks but nests on high, dry plains and plateaus and in semi-desert uplands. In Britain, curlews and golden plovers nest on moorland slopes and in marshy valleys. Lapwings nest in the valley fields.

Mountains are interesting because you can study the changes in weather, vegetation, and bird life as you climb higher. The habitats change in the same way as they would if you were traveling toward the poles, but much more quickly. By the time you reach the top of some high, windswept peaks, it feels like the Arctic—for you and the birds.

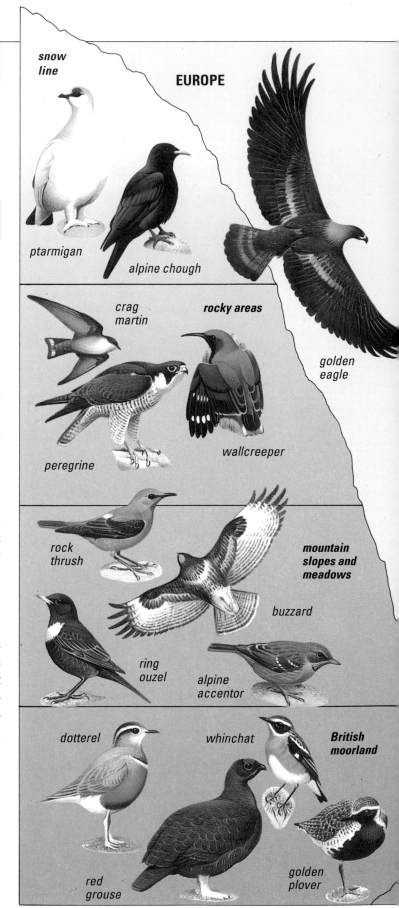

snow line

EUROPE

ptarmigan

alpine chough

golden eagle

rocky areas

crag martin

peregrine

wallcreeper

rock thrush

mountain slopes and meadows

buzzard

ring ouzel

alpine accentor

dotterel

whinchat

British moorland

red grouse

golden plover

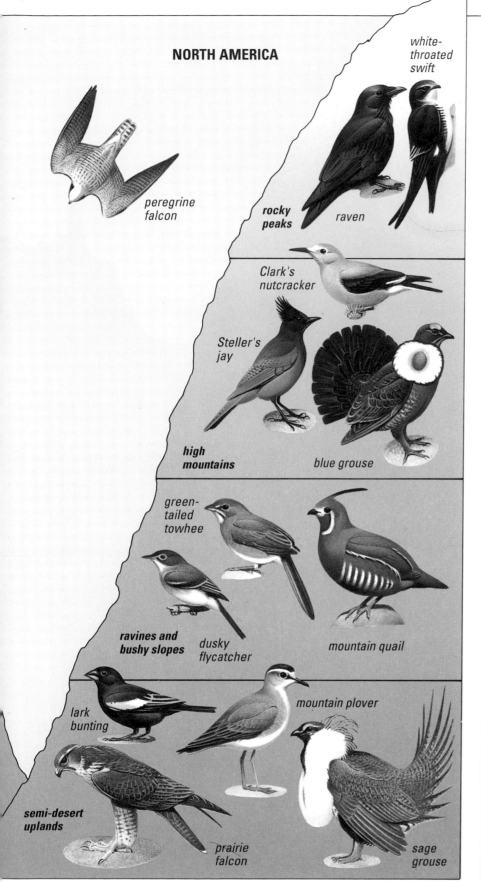

NORTH AMERICA

peregrine falcon

white-throated swift

rocky peaks

raven

Clark's nutcracker

Steller's jay

high mountains

blue grouse

green-tailed towhee

ravines and bushy slopes

dusky flycatcher

mountain quail

lark bunting

mountain plover

semi-desert uplands

prairie falcon

sage grouse

GAME BIRDS: PEAKS TO PLAINS

Game birds live in all upland habitats. The ptarmigan lives on the highest peaks and on the Arctic tundra. Willow grouse are Arctic birds of northern Scandinavia. Red grouse are birds of high British heather moors. Mountain quails live on high bushy slopes in the North American Rockies. Sage grouse prefer sagebrush in the foothills. Prairie chickens are rare and declining in the remnants of tall-grass prairies.

MOUNTAIN FIELDCRAFT

It is vital to be safe and comfortable on a hike in mountains and hills. Always go in a group, and tell someone where you are going and when you'll be back. Check the weather forecast, and never set off if bad weather is predicted. Wear warm, protective clothing and hiking boots and bring extra layers. Take plenty of food and drink, maps, and a compass. Be careful! Mountains can be dangerous.

ALWAYS VIGILANT
Be on the lookout for birds as soon as you get to the mountains. A few birds are relatively tame and can be found around parking lots. Juncos and black-capped chickadees are year-round mountain residents.

SOLID FOOTHOLDS
Never go close to the edges of cliffs or stony slopes that could give way beneath you. There will be plenty of safe paths and viewpoints on your route. Even grassy slopes can be slippery, so don't be tempted to creep down them.

ADVANCING YOUR HOBBY

The best and most expert birdwatchers live their whole lives aware of birds. They watch birds from the house, from the car, from trains, from the office. Birds are everywhere, so there is no chance to stop! You, too, can become a top birder or even an expert ornithologist—a scientist who studies birds—but it takes time to gain the knowledge and experience. If that is your aim, or if you simply enjoy watching birds for fun, there is no end to the ways you can advance your hobby—or your career!

GETTING INTO BIRD STUDIES

Birds are easy to find in the backyard or park or around a nearby lake. Perhaps you are near a reservoir or some woods. To begin your studies, set some goals, such as recording the seasonal changes or spotting all the species in a given area. The most important thing is to keep good notes of which birds you see, when they visit, how many there are, and so on. You can analyze your notes later.

A MARK OF DISTINCTION

Bewick's swans in England have been studied by making detailed drawings of their face patterns. Each bird is recognizable. Perhaps you can recognize some birds by their own individual marks.

Most local bird societies help to protect and develop habitats for birds and other wildlife—for example, by cutting scrub or clearing garbage from pondsides.

Cleaning oiled seabirds has to be done by an expert. Without their natural oils, the feathers become wet when the birds return to the water, and they drown or die of cold.

BIRD SONG STUDIES

A diary of bird song might be your project. You can relate it to the weather. Do birds sing earlier in the morning in spring or in autumn? Do more sing at dusk in the summer? There is a lot to be discovered.

If you observe birds singing and displaying, you can make maps of breeding birds in their territories. Maps are the tools of census work. They show symbols for each species and indicate whether males were seen singing, fighting, or displaying to females, or females were seen taking food to young. Conservation organizations throughout the world use such censuses to plan their efforts to protect wildlife.

MIGRATION WATCH

Woods and waterside places are great for seeing migrants arrive in spring. It is easy to record the first time you see each summer visitor every year. It is harder to record the last time! Keep a chart of migrant arrival and departure dates. Look at your local bird club reports to see how your dates compare with others. Send your notes in to the local recorder so they can be added to the reports.

These are just a few ideas. You will think of other exciting avenues to explore in your area. Whatever you do, have fun!

On many nature preserves, bird boxes are put up to attract birds to nest. The boxes are checked periodically to see if they are being used and to record the breeding numbers. *Never* look in bird boxes: at certain stages the parents will abandon the nest rather than defend it.

SOME PROJECT IDEAS

Check out nest sites of barn swallows. Which direction do they face? Are there more on white-painted house eaves than on any other color? If so, why? Do barn swallows like new houses or old ones?

Watch big gulls. You can see when they start to molt and when they finish many weeks later. Keep a chart of their molt timing. You will find that old birds molt at different times from young ones.

In autumn, birds eat berries. Find out what types of berries are around. See which birds choose which berries first, and which are left until later. What happens in winter if it snows?

Making maps of birds' territories is a good project. It is easiest to do this with birds which sing or display distinctively, or have eye-catching colors, such as this female stonechat on a prominent perch.

INDEX